The Gift

of

Peace

The Gift of Peace

of

Peace

PERSONAL
REFLECTIONS
BY

Joseph Cardinal Bernardin

 Loyola Press
CHICAGO

Loyola Press
3441 North Ashland Avenue
Chicago, Illinois 60657

Cover and interior design by Biner Design

Library of Congress Cataloging-in-Publication Data

Bernardin, Joseph Louis, 1928–96
    The gift of peace : personal reflections / by Joseph
Cardinal Bernardin.
    p.   cm.
    ISBN 0–8294–0955–6
    1. Bernardin, Joseph Louis, 1928–96. 2. Cardinals—
Illinois—Chicago Region—Biography. 3. Catholic
Church—Illinois—Chicago Region—Biography.
4. Chicago Region (Ill.)—Church history—20th century.
5. Death—Religious aspects—Catholic Church.
6. Spiritual life—Catholic Church.   I. Title.
BX4705.B38125A3   1997
282' .092—dc21
[B]   96-50335
                                            CIP

97 98 99 00 01 / 10 9 8 7 6 5 4 3 2 1

CONTENTS

AS THOSE WHO SERVE

Nov. 1, 1996

My dear friends,
     It is the feast of All
Saints and I am home
because the Pastoral Center of the
Archdiocese is closed. The
weather is much colder than
it was several days ago, but
it is still good for walking.
Normally, I would be doing
just that.

     But today I will not
do any walking. The reason is
that a pervasive fatigue —one
that is characteristic of pancreatic
cancer—has overtaken me.

Besides, I am still experiencing discomfort in my lower back and legs because of the spinal stenosis that was diagnosed about a year ago.

So, as I sit at my desk, I thought I would do something else. I have decided to write this very personal letter explaining why I have written this little book, _The Gift of Peace_. It is not an autobiography, but simply a reflection on my life and ministry during the past three years, years that have been as joyful as they have been difficult. My reflections begin with the allegation of sexual misconduct brought against me November 1993 and continue to the present as I prepare for the last stage of my life which began in June 1995 with the diagnosis of an aggressive form of cancer.

To paraphrase Charles Dickens in *A Tale of Two Cities,* "it has been the best of times, it has been the worst of times." The *worst* because of the humiliation, physical pain, anxiety and fear. The *best* because of the reconciliation, love, pastoral sensitivity and peace that have resulted from God's grace and the support and prayers of so many people. While not denying the former, this reflection focuses on the latter, showing how, if we let him, God can write straight with crooked lines. To put it another way, this reflection is intended to help others understand how the good and the bad are always present in our human condition and, that if we "let go," if we place ourselves totally in the hands of the Lord, the good will prevail.

On a very personal note, I invite those who read this book to walk with me the final miles of my life's journey. When we reach the gate, I will have to go in first — that seems to be the rule; one at a time by designation. But know that I will carry each of you in my heart! Ultimately, we will all be together, intimately united with the Lord Jesus whom we love so much.

Peace and love,
Joseph Card. Bernardin

ACKNOWLEDGMENTS

THIS BOOK COVERS the last three years of my life. So many people have played an important role in my life during this very difficult time—family and friends, staff and colleagues, attorneys and doctors, priests and fellow cancer patients—that it is quite impossible for me to thank them all by name. But I am eternally grateful to all of them for their many kindnesses.

In regard to this book, I am very grateful to my longtime friend, Dr. Eugene Kennedy, who helped me launch this project in early September and was both generous and gracious in reviewing and responding to the drafts of my introduction and first two chapters.

I am also grateful to Father Al Spilly, C.PP.S., my special assistant over the last twelve and a half years, and to Mr. Jeremy Langford, managing editor in charge of acquisitions at Loyola Press, for helping me bring this special book to completion. I add a special word of thanks to Mrs. Marie Feller Knoll, communications associate on my personal staff, for her assistance as well.

Finally, I acknowledge my longtime friend and associate, Monsignor Kenneth Velo, without whose daily understanding and support I could never have completed this and many other projects of the last three years in particular.

INTRODUCTION

Letting Go

LETTING GO

THROUGHOUT MY SPIRITUAL JOURNEY I have struggled to become closer to God. As I prepare now for my passage from this world into the next, I cannot help but reflect on my life and recognize the themes that, like old friends, have been so important to me all these years. One theme that rises to the surface more than any other takes on new meaning for me now—the theme of letting go.

By letting go, I mean the ability to release from our grasp those things that inhibit us from developing an intimate relationship with the Lord Jesus.

Letting go is never easy. Indeed, it is a lifelong process. But letting go is possible if we understand the importance of opening our hearts and, above all else, developing a healthy prayer life. It has taken me a lifetime to learn these truths, but I want to share with you some background and one story that always stands out as a pivotal point in my life.

I entered the seminary when I was only seventeen years old, and ever since then I have been trying to learn how to pray. In those early years, I was under the spiritual care of the Sulpician Fathers, both at St. Mary's Seminary in Baltimore and Theological College at Catholic University. They had a special routine that brought us together in the evening to give us points for reflection. In the morning before Mass, we would all gather in what was known as the Prayer Hall to do the reflection. There were times when I wondered whether this was the best form of teaching, but I have to say in retrospect that it certainly introduced me to the importance of prayer and the fact that prayer is not a one-sided practice. Rather, prayer involves speaking and listening on both sides.

After my ordination in 1952, I probably prayed as much as any busy young priest of those days. But in the mid-1970s, I discovered that I was giving a higher priority to good works than to prayer. I was telling others—seminarians, priests, lay people, and religious—about the importance of prayer, emphasizing that they could not really be connected with the Lord unless they prayed. But I felt somewhat hypocritical in my teaching because I was not setting aside adequate time for personal prayer. It was not that I lacked the desire to pray or that I had suddenly decided prayer was not important. Rather, I was very busy, and I fell into the trap of thinking that my good works were more important than prayer.

One evening during this time I spoke to three priests with whom I was having dinner. All three were younger than I, and I had ordained two of them myself since going to Cincinnati in 1972. During the conversation I told them that I was finding it difficult to pray and asked if they could help me. I'm not sure that I was totally honest when I asked for their help because I didn't know whether I would be willing to do what they suggested. "Are you sincere in what you request? Do you really want to turn this around?" they asked. What could I say? I couldn't say no after what I had just told them!

In very direct—even blunt terms—they helped me realize that as a priest and a bishop I was urging a spirituality on others that I was not fully practicing myself. That was a turning point in my life. These priests helped me understand that you

have to give what they called, and what many
spiritual directors today call, "quality time" to
prayer. It can't be done "on the run." You have to
put aside good time, quality time. After all, if we
believe that the Lord Jesus is the Son of God, then
of all persons to whom we give of ourselves, we
should give him the best we have.

I decided to give God the first hour of my day,
no matter what, to be with him in prayer and
meditation where I would try to open the door
even wider to his entrance. This put my life in a
new and uplifting perspective; I also found that I
was able to share the struggles of my own spiritual
journey with others. Knowing that I went through
the same things they did gave them great encouragement. This has become a crucial element of my
ministry with cancer patients and others who are
seriously ill.

Still, letting go is never easy. I have prayed and
struggled constantly to be able to let go of things
more willingly, to be free of everything that keeps
the Lord from finding greater hospitality in my
soul or interferes with my surrender to what God
asks of me.

It is clear that God wants me to let go now.
But there is something in us humans that makes

us want to hold onto ourselves and everything and everybody familiar to us. My daily prayer is that I can open wide the doors of my heart to Jesus and his expectations of me.

So I now let go more freely, delivered by the Lord from the frustration I sometimes experienced even when I tried before, as earnestly as I could, to break free from the grip of things. I have reflected on Zacchaeus, the tax collector whose story is told in the Gospel of Luke. When he received Jesus into his house, some people complained that Jesus had gone to the home of a sinner. Zacchaeus "stood his ground and said to the Lord, 'I give half my belongings, Lord, to the poor. If I have defrauded anyone in the past, I pay him back fourfold.' And Jesus replied, 'Today salvation has come to this house for this is what it means to be a son of Abraham. The Son of Man has come to search out and save what was lost'" (Cf. Lk 19:1–10).

I have desperately wanted to open the door of my soul as Zacchaeus opened the door of his house. Only in that way can the Lord take over my life completely. Yet many times in the past I have only let him come in part of the way. I talked with him but seemed afraid to let him take over.

Why was I afraid? Why did I open the door only so far and no more? I have searched my soul for answers. At times, I think it was because I wanted to succeed and be acknowledged as a person who has succeeded. At other times I would become upset when I read or heard criticism about my decisions or actions. When these feelings prevailed, I wanted to control things, that is, I wanted to make them come out "right." When I reacted that way, I tended not to put full confidence in people until they had proven themselves to me.

I found that on occasion I have dealt with the Lord in the same way. Conceptually, I understand that he can and should be trusted. I remind myself that it is his Church, that nothing happens beyond his purview. Still, knowing all that, I often found that I would hold back, unwilling to let go completely.

Have I feared that God's will may be different from mine and that if his will prevailed I would be criticized? Or was there another reason? Perhaps, psychologically and emotionally, I have simply been unable to let go.

Part of the reason for my reluctance was the fact that every day so many people made demands on me. Their expectations were so numerous, so diverse and personal that I could not seem to free myself as fully as I would have liked from these pressures.

I have also asked whether it was simply pride that haunted me, making me unwilling to take the risk of letting go. Or did I sometimes feel almost paralyzed because I was, in a way, whipsawed by groups in the Church that competed for my attention and support, those who saw themselves as progressive who wanted me to carry their banners and those who saw themselves as conserving tradition who expected me to be loyal to them? Each had a genuine claim, yet I felt I had to try in everything to do what is right for the whole Church. Sometimes the resulting tension caused me to be cautious in expressing what I really thought.

To come at this in another way, I wonder if I refused to let the Lord enter all the way into my soul because I feared that he would insist that, in my personal life, I let go of certain things that I was reluctant or unwilling to give up. These were the ordinary things, I knew, and most of them had been gifts from others. Still, I recognized that I could be attached to them.

More than fifteen years ago I gave away all the money I had and said that I would never again have a savings account or stocks. I pledged that I would keep only what was needed to maintain my checking account. I began depositing almost all the monetary gifts in a special account of the Archdiocese that is used for personal charities and special projects of various kinds. Nonetheless, I have received so many gifts in the last few years that I began to save some for myself, using the argument that I might need the funds in retirement or for my aged mother. I have now reexamined all this and ensured that I am free from things so that I am no longer distracted in my relationship with the Lord.

In recent years, as I struggled to let go, I wondered whether God was preparing me for something special—or whether the struggle was only a part of normal spiritual development. It is certainly part of the latter. But now I know that Jesus was preparing me for something special.

The past three years have taught me a great deal about myself and my relationship to God, the Church, and others. Three major events within these years have led me to where I am today. First, the false accusation of sexual misconduct in November 1993 and my eventual reconciliation with my accuser a year later. Second, the diagnosis of pancreatic cancer in June 1995 and the surgery that rendered me "cancer free" for fifteen months. And third, the cancer's return at the end of August 1996, this time in the liver, and my decision to discontinue chemotherapy one month later and live the rest of my life as fully as possible.

Within these major events lies the story of my life—what I have believed and who I have worked hard to be. And because of the nature of these events, I have deepened and developed my own spirituality and gained insights that I want to share. By no means are these reflections meant to be a comprehensive autobiography. They are simply reflections from my heart to yours. I hope they will be of help to you in your own life so you too can enjoy the deep inner peace—God's wonderful gift to me—that I now embrace as I stand on the threshold of eternal life.

PART ONE

False
Accusation

Emptying Oneself

GOD SPEAKS VERY GENTLY to us when he invites us to make more room for him in our lives. The tension that arises comes not from him but from me as I struggle to find out *how* to offer him fuller hospitality and then to *do* it wholeheartedly. The Lord is clear about what he wants, but it is really difficult to let go of myself and my work and trust him completely. The first step of letting go, of course, is linked with my *emptying* myself of everything—the plans I consider the largest as well as the distractions I judge the smallest—so that the Lord really can take over.

St. Paul's description of Jesus' mission is never far from my thoughts: "Though he was in the form of God, he did not deem equality with God something to be grasped at. Rather, he emptied himself and took the form of a slave, being born in the likeness of men. He was known to be of human estate, and it was thus that he humbled himself, obediently accepting death, death on a cross" (Phil 2:6–8).

To close the gap between what I am and what God wants of me, I must empty myself and let Jesus come in and take over. I have prayed to understand his agenda for me. Some things stand out. He wants me to focus on the *essentials* of his message and way of life rather than on the accidentals that needlessly occupy so much of our time and efforts. One can easily distinguish essentials from peripherals in the spiritual life. Essentials ask us to give true witness and to love others more. Nonessentials close us in on ourselves.

It is unsettling to pray to be emptied of self; it seems a challenge almost beyond our reach as humans. But if we try, I have learned, God does most of the work. I must simply let myself go in love and trust of the Lord.

When the hand of God's purpose enters my life, however, it is usually not from the front, as I have always expected, but from the side, in murmurs and whispers that not only surprise but soon empty me beyond anything I could imagine.

FACING FALSE CHARGES

O N WEDNESDAY, November 10, 1993, I was in New York to give the annual Thomas Merton Lecture at Columbia University. Cardinal John O'Connor, with whom I was staying, told me of a disturbing rumor that was circulating: A U.S. Cardinal was to be accused of sex abuse. Its source was uncertain, and its vagueness made it seem unworthy and yet ominous at the same time.

The rumors were growing by the time I returned to my office the next day. I was stunned to learn that some people were speculating that I was the Cardinal to be accused. In phone calls from friends, I discovered that rumors about an impending lawsuit were spreading rapidly across the country and around the world. I would be served papers the next morning charging that, when I was Archbishop of Cincinnati, I sexually abused a seminarian.

The accusation startled and devastated me. I tried to get beyond the unconfirmed rumors and return to my work, but this lurid charge against

my deepest ideals and commitments kept consum-
ing my attention. Indeed, I could think of little
else as my aides continued to bring me additional
details of rumors that were still circulating. I sat
quietly for a moment and asked myself a simple
question: Was this what the Lord had been
preparing me for, to face false accusations about
something that I knew never took place? Spurious
charges, I realized, were what Jesus himself experienced. But this evolving nightmare seemed
completely unreal. It did not seem possible that
this was happening to me.

Late in the afternoon, Mary Ann Ahern of the
local NBC television affiliate called, saying she
had had a copy of the allegations read to her, that
the plaintiff's name was Steven and that he was
represented by a New Jersey lawyer who special-
ized in suing the clergy for sexual abuse. The
lawsuit was to be filed in Cincinnati the next
morning. "They claim to have pictures of Steven
and the Cardinal together," the reporter read from
the information that was surfacing in newsrooms
across the country.

We learned a few minutes later that Steven's
last name was Cook. I searched my memory for a

face to go with the name Steven Cook. None appeared. "He was a college student at Saint Gregory's," a staff member informed me, "and now he's in his mid-thirties and is very ill with AIDS. That's all we know."

Steven Cook. I still could not conjure up a face to go with the name of this person who, according to what was now a full-blown storm of rumor, claimed that he was led to my bedroom in 1975 and forced to submit to a sex act. Who, in God's name, was this person, and why was he accusing me of something that he must have known, as I did, never took place? I then recalled hearing that this same person had already brought complaints to the Archdiocese of Cincinnati against a priest who was on the faculty of St. Gregory's Seminary there. I began to surmise that because, in Steven's judgment, he had not received a satisfactory response from Cincinnati, his lawyer had decided to bring me into the case since I was Archbishop at the time. Later, Steven would tell me how this came about.

I thought of my sincere prayer to learn to let go and empty myself. Was God's answer hidden in this lawsuit through which faceless accusers threatened to brand me indelibly as a sex abuser, a charge that has been leveled at many priests in recent years? Before most other dioceses, I oversaw the development of the first comprehensive guidelines for processing sexual abuse charges against priests of the Archdiocese of Chicago. The procedures were widely adopted throughout the country. One of my first actions in the face of this accusation would be to refer these charges against me to the review board that was part of this process.

I felt a deep humiliation as inquiring callers made it clear that the accusation had now circled the world, that millions of people would know only one thing about me, that I was charged with abusing the trust and the body of a minor almost twenty years before. My advisers urged me to issue a statement to the media whose trucks, which I could see from my office window, were crowding against each other on Superior Street below.

But how do you say anything about a charge you have not seen from persons you do not know about something you did not do? As never before,

I felt the presence of evil. From deep in my soul, however, I heard the Lord's words that calmed the storm breaking around and within me: "The truth will set you free" (Jn 8:32).

I immediately wrote the following statement: "While I have not seen the suit and I do not know the details of the allegation, there is one thing I do know, and I state categorically: I have never abused anyone in all my life, anywhere, any time, any place."

The truth, I decided, was the only defense I had. After giving my statement to the waiting reporters, I drove home through streets that seemed familiar and yet changed, as I myself had been, by the events of the day.

The truth will set you free. I believed that, and I trusted the Lord who, for reasons I could not yet fathom, had permitted this trial to enter my life. But I also wondered if the voice of truth could be heard in a culture in which image making and distortion have almost completely replaced it. My faith reassured me that the truth was all that I had, and all that I really needed. It would be my rod and my staff through the dark valley (Ps 23:4) in the months ahead.

SHARING THE TRUTH
WITH THE WORLD

THE SIMPLE TRUTH is that I was innocent of the charges against me. This sustained me on a night filled with phone calls and the breaking news on all the Chicago TV channels at 10:00 P.M. that I had been accused of abusing Steven Cook. Only Bill Kurtis of the local CBS television affiliate raised the possibility that another story might lie beneath this one, that certain people might be out to "get" Cardinal Bernardin. I had critics, I knew, but I could not imagine who would resort to these tactics to harm me. A friend called that evening and told me he suspected a conspiracy. I told him that this had already crossed my mind.

I was angry and bewildered that people who did not know me would make such destructive charges against me. There seemed to be some calculation involved because these accusations could not be construed as some innocent misunderstanding of facts. My first worry was about the impact that these imputations of my character would have on the Church. The attack was directed against the most important thing I had going for me as a religious leader, my reputation. If my credibility was destroyed, so was my ability to lead. If my people believed I could do what I was charged with doing, how could they place their trust in me? And would they trust me during that period in which the charges hung over my head and my office?

I decided to face the next day with faith in the truth. I could not help thinking that I was not the only one caught up in those false charges. My intuition was that the young man described as my accuser might have been drawn somehow into this himself. I had no facts to support that sense of his being a pawn in this terrible game, but I felt it clearly. If I was right, he needed prayers as much as I did right then. I felt a genuine impulse to pray with and comfort him.

Indeed, I put those heartfelt feelings into a letter written to him a few days after the filing of the case. I learned much later that his lawyer never passed it on to him. It read, in part:

> . . . as I thought it over, I began to think
> that you must be suffering a great deal.

The idea came to me yesterday morning
that it would be a good thing if I visited
with you personally. The purpose of the
visit would be strictly pastoral—to show
my concern for you and to pray with you.
If you are interested in such a visit, please
let me know. I will come to you if you wish.

The next morning, Friday, November 12,
the allegations against me were the lead stories
in the press of almost every large city in the
world. As I prayed the rosary early in the
morning, I meditated on the first of the sorrowful mysteries, the Agony in the Garden. I
said to the Lord, "In all my sixty-five years, this
is the first time that I have really understood
the pain and agony you felt that night." And I
also asked, "Why did you let this happen?" I
had never felt more alone.

I spent most of my morning meeting with my
advisers, preparing for the press conference that
was scheduled for 1:00 P.M. My morale was
boosted by the letters and calls of support that had
already begun to arrive, including a supportive
statement from the Holy See.

My counselors discussed all aspects of the case as well as the strategies to use in handling them. We learned that CNN was airing promotional pieces every hour for a Sunday night special entitled "Fall from Grace" about priests who were found guilty of sex crimes. The promotional piece promised an interview with Steven Cook. He and the reporter were shown examining what they called "evidence" against me—a book and a picture. Because this interview had already been conducted and the show scheduled to air on the eve of the semiannual meeting of the National Conference of Catholic Bishops, it seemed that a good measure of planning had gone into developing the "case" against me.

At the conclusion of the meeting with my advisers, I decided to take an hour by myself to pray and reflect. I was being emptied of self in a way that I never could have anticipated, and I wanted to let go and place myself and my cares in the hands of the Lord. I was conscious of the blur of everyday life in the great city outside my windows and of the arrival once more of the caravan of media trucks in the street below. Ten minutes before the scheduled press conference I called an old friend and said, "I have been listening to good advice from good people all morning. I have made a decision to follow my own instincts. I am just going to tell the truth."

Electricity filled the conference room of the Pastoral Center where almost seventy reporters were jammed together in a tangle of cameras, lights, and trailing wires. I understood that these journalists, many of whom I knew and liked, had to assume adversarial roles to carry out their work. But I was not there to do battle with them. I just wanted to answer truthfully their questions.

But as I moved behind the brace of micro-phones, I felt that I was literally standing before the entire world, and I still felt very much alone. The most important thing I had going for me at the moment was my forty-two years of ordained ministry, my name, and my reputation. But there was also an inner strength, and I am convinced that the Lord was giving me that strength. For me, this moment of public accusation and inquiry was also a moment of grace. A moment of pain, but a moment of grace because I felt the great love and support that many people were giving me. Above all, it was a moment of spiritual growth. I felt that

I was entering a new phase of my spiritual journey because of the events of those few days.

Midway into the session, the tension in the room lessened somewhat. While the atmosphere remained grave, it appeared that the truth, as the Lord promised, was freeing me and, in turn, changing the attitudes of those asking me questions. They seemed less doubting, less hostile, more ready to believe than to disbelieve me. Still, their job was to probe and provoke.

The tension reappeared in the waning moments of the press conference when a young man in the front row asked me, "Are you sexually active?"

I paused only a moment, feeling briefly the enormous gulf between the reporter's world and my own. "I have always led," I said simply, "a chaste and celibate life." The reinstated tightness in the atmosphere loosened, and I could read in the eyes of the assembled journalists that they believed me. Afterwards, one told me, "We know now that you're telling the truth, Cardinal, but we have to ask these questions. Our job depends on it." The next day's headline in the *Chicago Tribune* read, " 'I've Led a Chaste Life,' Bernardin Says."

After the session ended, I returned to my office. If it was an ordeal, I thought to myself, it was only the first of many. Indeed, I was to hold fourteen press conferences over the next week, all of them governed by the same dynamics. The truth, as faith promises, did earn me a greater sense of freedom at each of these meetings.

THE CASE UNRAVELS

IT TOOK ONE HUNDRED DAYS before the false charges against me were resolved. They may be described as an education in law, but I prefer to think of them as a profound education of the soul. The entire matter really served as scenes in the first act of a three-act play that I now believe constitutes my spiritual pilgrimage over the past three years. This first act began with the false accusation and concluded with my meeting my accuser and reconciling with him. The other two acts, which I will discuss in detail later in this book, include the diagnosis of my pancreatic cancer and my preparation for death. At the time of the accusation, I was only at the beginning of a three-year schooling of the Spirit, but as the year drew to an end I could not fully foresee that.

From the very beginning, even though I knew that I would have to defend myself and the Church in a way that would be successful, I told my lawyers that I wanted no countersuit, that we would not pursue a "scorched earth" policy. The reason was that I did not want to deter persons who had really been abused from coming forward.

I also determined early on that I would not spend any archdiocesan money in my defense for fear that that would be used by some people as an excuse *not* to contribute to the Church. As soon as this became known, a number of prestigious law firms came forward, offering to defend me on a *pro bono* basis, including the firm we were already using for various legal matters.

As soon as the alleged "evidence" was examined, the case against me began to collapse from within. Indeed, the "picture" of me and the plaintiff turned out to be a group photograph taken at a Cincinnati seminary function at which, along with many others, we were both present. The book I allegedly autographed and gave to him bore no signature of mine. The "hypnotist" who supposedly helped the plaintiff, just a month before, to recall memories of my sexually abusing him was found to be someone who had taken only a few hours of training in hypnotism. Moreover, I later learned that she was unaware of the real reason Steven had been sent to her.

It became clear to me that certain critics of mine had played a role in urging Steven Cook to take on the role of plaintiff against me. Indeed, almost as soon as the news broke, some people, including a priest from out of state, expressed the opinion on a local radio talk show that I was guilty, that finally the facts had caught up with me. Also, the night between the publication of the rumor and the filing of the case, a significant section of the telephones at the archdiocesan Pastoral Center was "invaded." Six different messages were left on the phones and were heard the next morning by the staff in the various offices affected. The theme of all six was that I was guilty of the rumored charge and that it would not be to the advantage of the Archdiocese to defend me. Later efforts to find out who did this were not successful.

Under the professional discipline of my lawyers, principally John O'Malley and James

Serritella, the true nature of the case against me quickly became apparent. Despite its unfounded nature, this lawsuit possessed the power both to disrupt and to change the direction of my life.

As the disturbing allegations did not stand the test of truth, I began to understand how Steven Cook had been a victim of this whole tawdry episode. My initial intuition of his being used was gradually confirmed. On February 28, 1994, Steven on his own initiative asked a judge at the federal court in Cincinnati to drop the charges against me.

More striking to me than the fact that a troubled priest at St. Gregory Seminary had unwittingly played a role in promoting my false indictment was what we gradually learned of Steven Cook's own difficult life. His brief unhappy period in the Cincinnati seminary had been followed by an estrangement from the Church and a drift into a promiscuous lifestyle. He was suffering from AIDS and was being cared for by a friend at an apartment in Philadelphia whose address they kept secret. He was the sheep who had been lost, and, as a shepherd, I knew that I had to seek him out.

MEETING MY ACCUSER:
FORGIVENESS
AND RECONCILIATION

INDEED, AFTER THE CASE WAS DROPPED and my
final press conference on the matter was covered
by the same CNN that had played such a promi-
nent part in publicizing the initial accusation,
I plunged back into my crowded schedule.
Nonetheless, I thought often of Steven in his
lonely, illness-ridden exile from both his parental
home and the Church. By mid-December I felt
deeply that this entire episode would not be complete until I followed my shepherd's calling to seek
him out. I only prayed that he would receive me.
The experience of the false accusation would not
be complete until I met and reconciled with
Steven. Even though I had never heard from him,
I sensed he also wanted to see me.

Not knowing his address or phone number
and not wanting to take him by surprise, I made
contact with Steven's mother, Mary, through
Father Phil Seher, her pastor in Cincinnati and a
friend of mine. She sent back word that Steven

was not only willing but also had a real desire to meet with me. I flew to Philadelphia with Father Scott Donahue on December 30, 1994. Monsignor James Malloy, the rector of St. Charles Borromeo Seminary, where the meeting was to be held, picked us up and drove us to its campus in suburban Overbrook.

I was a bit anxious as we entered the snow-patched seminary grounds. The campus, with its traditional granite structures, was quiet—the seminarians were on Christmas vacation. In the large, tall-windowed room on the second floor of the main building, we waited patiently for Steven and his companion. It was hard to refrain from asking myself an unwelcome question: Would Steven be able to keep the appointment or not?

Within a few minutes he arrived with his friend, Kevin. We shook hands, and I sat with Steven on a couch as Father Donahue and Kevin sat in the wing chairs at either end of it. Steven looked only slightly gaunt despite his grave illness. I explained to him that the only reason for requesting the meeting was to bring closure to the traumatic events of last winter by personally letting him know that I harbored no ill feelings toward him. I told him I wanted to pray with him for his physical and spiritual well-being. Steven replied that he had decided to meet with me so he could apologize for the embarrassment and hurt he had caused. In other words, we both sought reconciliation. However, Steven said he wanted to tell me about his life before we continued.

With a tone and gestures that indicated Steven had bottled up his story for a long time, he told me that as a young seminarian he had been sexually abused by a priest he thought was his friend. He claimed that the authorities did not take his report of the priest's misconduct seriously. He became embittered and left the Church. Much later, he came into contact with a New Jersey–based lawyer with a reputation for bringing legal actions against priests accused of sexual abuse. This lawyer, Steven said, put him in touch with a priest in another state to advise him spiritually.

Although Steven was pursuing a case only against his seminary teacher, his priest adviser began mentioning me, Cardinal Bernardin, suggesting that, if I were included in the case, Steven would surely get back what he wanted from the Church. This "spiritual guide" pushed my name,

urging Steven to name me along with the other
priest in the legal action. He also urged Steven's
mother to cooperate in this plan, sending her
flowers as part of his effort to persuade her to support Steven's action. This was the very same priest
who expressed his opinion during a Chicago radio
talk show on November 12, 1993, that I was guilty.

It became difficult for Steven to explain how,
with what he described as a poorly trained thera-
pist, he thought that he had recaptured memories
of my abusing him and went along with including
me in the suit. He seemed confused and uncertain
about this. His friend Kevin broke in to say that
he was always suspicious of the lawyer and the
priest adviser.

I looked directly at Steven, seated a few inches
away from me. "You know," I said, "that I never
abused you."

"I know," he answered softly. "Can you tell me
that again?"

I looked directly into his eyes. "I have never
abused you. You know that, don't you?"

Steven nodded. "Yes," he replied, "I know
that, and I want to apologize for saying that you
did." Steven's apology was simple, direct, deeply

moving. I accepted his apology. I told him that I had prayed for him every day and would continue to pray for his health and peace of mind. It became increasingly clear that he was in precarious health.

I then asked whether he wanted me to celebrate Mass for him. At first, he hesitated. "I'm not sure I want to have Mass," he said haltingly; "I've felt very alienated from God and the Church a long time." He said that on several occasions while in a hotel he threw a Gideon Bible against the wall in anger and frustration. "Perhaps," he said, "just a simple prayer would be more appropriate."

I hesitated for a moment after that, unsure of how he would react to the gift I removed from my briefcase. I told him that I would not press the issue but did want to show him two items I had brought with me. "Steven," I said, "I have brought you something, a Bible that I have inscribed to you. But I do understand, and I won't be offended if you don't want to accept it." Steven took the Bible in quivering hands, pressed it to his heart as tears welled up in his eyes.

I then took a hundred-year-old chalice out of my case. "Steven, this is a gift from a man I don't even know. He asked me to use it to say Mass for you some day."

"Please," Steven responded tearfully, "let's celebrate Mass now."

Never in my entire priesthood have I witnessed a more profound reconciliation. The words I am using to tell you this story cannot begin to describe the power of God's grace at work that afternoon. It was a manifestation of God's love, forgiveness, and healing that I will never forget.

Kevin, Steven's friend, asked if he, a non-Catholic, could attend, and I told him that it would be fine. We all went to the seminary chapel where, with great joy and thanksgiving, Father Donahue and I celebrated Mass for the Feast of the Holy Family. We all embraced at the greeting of peace, and, afterwards, I anointed Steven with the sacrament of the sick.

Then I said a few words: "In every family there are times when there is hurt, anger, or alienation. But we cannot run away from our family. We have only one family and so, after every falling out, we must make every effort to be reconciled. So, too, the Church is our spiritual family. Once we become a member, we may be hurt or become alienated, but it is still our family. Since there is no other, we must work at reconciliation. And that is what we have been doing this very afternoon."

Before Steven left, he told me, "A big burden has been lifted from me today. I feel healed and very much at peace." We had previously agreed to keep our meeting secret, but Steven now said to me, "I'm so happy, I want people to know about our reconciliation." He asked me to tell the story, which I did a few weeks later in *The New World*, our archdiocesan paper. When I read it to him beforehand on the phone, he told me, "Cardinal, you're a good writer. Go with it."

As we flew back to Chicago that evening, Father Donahue and I felt the lightness of spirit that an afternoon of grace brings to one's life. I could not help but think that the ordeal of the accusation led straight to this extraordinary experience of God's grace in our sacramental reconciliation. And I could not help but recall the work of the Good Shepherd: to seek and restore to the sheepfold the one that has been, only for a while, lost.

Steven and I kept in touch after that and, six months later, when I received a diagnosis of pancreatic cancer, his was one of the first letters I received. He had only a few months to live when he wrote it, filled with sympathy and encouragement for me. He planned to visit me in Chicago at the end of August, but he was too ill. Steven died at his mother's home on September 22, 1995, fully reconciled with the Church. "This," he said, smiling from his deathbed at his mother about his return to the sacraments, "is my gift to you." The priest in Cincinnati who attended him told this to me soon afterwards.

PART TWO

Cancer

MEDITATION

Suffering in Communion with the Lord

THROUGHOUT MY MINISTRY I have focused on Jesus—his message, the events of his life, his relationship to the world. Now more than ever I focus on his cross, his suffering, which was not only real but also redemptive and life-giving.

Jesus was human. He felt pain as we do. And in many ways he experienced pain and suffering more deeply than we will ever know. Yet in the face of it all, he transformed human suffering into something greater: an ability to walk with the afflicted and to empty himself so that his loving Father could work more fully through him.

As we look upon the cross and recall the specific ways by which people share in its mystery, there are many perspectives to be considered. I will highlight only one: The essential mystery of the cross is that it gives rise to a certain kind of loneliness, an inability to see clearly how things are unfolding, an inability to see that, ultimately, all things will work for our good, and that we are, indeed, not alone.

This sense of being abandoned, this extreme experience of loneliness, is evident in Jesus' cry: "My God, my God, why have you forsaken me?" (Mt 27:46). If the Lord experienced pain and suffering, can we, as his disciples, expect anything less? No! Like Jesus, we too must expect pain. There is, however, a decisive difference between our pain as disciples and that experienced by those who are *not* the Lord's disciples. The difference stems from the fact that, as disciples, we suffer *in communion with* the Lord. And that makes all the difference in the world! Nevertheless, even this communion does not totally extinguish the loneliness, the sense of abandonment, no more than it did for Jesus.

Our understanding of suffering—not merely its inevitability but also its purpose and redemptive value—greatly impacts our ministry of presence. As a matter of fact, suffering severely tests us in this regard, and the reason is quite simple. Whenever we are with people who suffer, it frequently becomes evident that there is very little we can do to help them other than be present to them, walk with them as the Lord walks with us. The reason this is so frustrating is that we like to be "fixers." We want not only to control our own destiny but also that of others. So we are frustrated when all we can do for suffering persons is be present to them, pray with them—become, in effect, a silent sign of God's presence and love.

And yet, the ability to offer that kind of prayerful response is the key that unlocks the mystery of suffering. For, in the final analysis, our participation in the paschal mystery—in the suffering, death, and resurrection of Jesus—brings a certain *freedom*: the freedom to let go, to surrender ourselves to the living God, to place ourselves completely in his hands, knowing that ultimately he will win out! The more we cling to ourselves and others, the more we try to control our destiny—the more we lose the true sense of our lives, the more we are impacted by the futility of it all. It's precisely in letting go, in entering into complete union with the Lord, in letting him take over, that we discover our true selves. It's in the act of abandonment that we experience redemption, that we find life, peace, and joy in the midst of physical, emotional, and spiritual suffering.

This is the lesson we must first learn from Jesus before we can teach it to others. We must let the mystery, the tranquillity, and the purposefulness of Jesus' suffering become part of our own life before we can become effective instruments in the hands of the Lord for the sake of others.

As Christians, if we are to love as Jesus loved, we must first come to terms with suffering. Like Jesus, we simply cannot be cool and detached from our fellow human beings. Our years of living as Christians will be years of suffering for and with other people. Like Jesus, we will love others only if we walk with them in the valley of darkness—the dark valley of sickness, the dark valley of moral dilemmas, the dark valley of oppressive structures and diminished rights.

New Life

FOLLOWING THE DEEPLY MOVING and life-changing events of the previous year, I began 1995 as a liberated man. A great weight had been lifted from my shoulders, and I felt freer than ever before. Part of me wanted to write about the period of my false accusation, but after a great deal of prayer I decided simply to move forward with my life. God's grace had helped me both survive that trying time and deepen my understanding of what it means to forgive even those who hurt us most. During those months I emptied myself more than I ever had so that God could take over. As a result, my reconciliation with Steven Cook filled me with new life, and his request that I share our story with the world was record enough. It was time to take all that I had learned from the experience and continue my ministry with renewed energy and confidence.

Friends and staff members noticed the change and commented on how much I was taking on. For the first time in almost a year I could resume certain projects that had been postponed

or canceled. And in the midst of the exhilaration
I felt in catching up, I had to prepare for a very
full schedule in the months ahead.

Between January and March I made three
international trips. I began with a trip to the
Philippines for the first international meeting of
the Religious Alliance Against Pornography
(RAAP), of which I am one of the co-founders
and co-chairs. Our organization had achieved
some success in sensitizing the public to the terrible evil of child pornography, and people in
other countries requested our help. We decided
to host an international conference and chose
Manila as the meeting place because there is so
much child abuse, child pornography, and child
prostitution around the Pacific Rim. The meeting was quite successful.

Then in February I went to Australia and New
Zealand at the request of some bishops who
wanted me to give a series of lectures on various
ecclesial matters such as the future of the Church
in the third millennium, young people and their
relationship to the Church, tolerance in society
and the Church, as well the consistent ethic of life.
It was the first time that I had been to those two

countries, so I looked forward to going. It was a delightful experience. Fortunately there was a little time off between the lectures, and so I had a chance to see some of both countries. While I was traveling, I continued to thank God for my new energy and renewed dedication to my ministry.

The highlight of this period of travel came in March when I led a delegation of Catholics and Jews from Chicago to Israel, my first trip to the Holy Land. We were celebrating together more than twenty-five years of dialogue between the Catholic and Jewish communities in Chicago. By visiting together Israel, the West Bank, and Gaza, we hoped to share the experience of seeing first-hand the place of our respective religious origins as well as to model for others how Jews and Catholics can get along.

On March 20, just hours before I left for the airport, I ordained three new auxiliary bishops in Holy Name Cathedral. After that wonderful ceremony I embarked on what turned out to be an extraordinary trip. The media were very much interested in our trip, and all the major television stations, newspapers, and radio stations publicized it back home. The publicity, the articles, were very

positive. On that ten-day trip, the delegation and
I met with the Latin Patriarch of Jerusalem
Michel Sabbah, Israeli President Ezer Weizman,
Israeli Prime Minister Yitzhak Rabin, Israeli
Foreign Minister Shimon Peres, Mayor Elias Freij
of Bethlehem, Greek Orthodox Patriarch
Diodorus I, President of the Palestinian Authority
Yasir Arafat, the Apostolic Nuncio Archbishop
Cordero Lanza Di Montezemolo Andrea, and
Mayor Ehud Olmert of Jerusalem. There were
tensions at times in some of the discussions, but
we were very well received.

Because this trip to the Holy Land was so
powerful, I decided that I would return some day
as a pilgrim—that is, privately. Because of the
many public appearances—always in the full view
of the media—I didn't have a chance to spend
much time in the places where Jesus lived and
ministered. I determined then that I would return.
I had every intention of doing so, but now that is
not going to happen. I savor the memories and
feelings from the little that I saw of the places
where Jesus lived, ministered, and died. I have a
better understanding of the Scriptures and the
images used in them.

When we returned from Israel, I prepared for Easter. It seemed so appropriate to celebrate the mystery of Jesus' death and resurrection at this time in my life. I, too, had been resurrected, from the depths of a serious false accusation. The mystery of Jesus' triumph over such great pain and sorrow at the end of his life now made more sense to me. As I had done so many times before, I spent the days leading up to Easter in the quiet hours of the morning praying intensely that I might come to understand more of Jesus so that I could be more effective in my work as a priest, as a bishop.

The hectic pace of my ministry continued through May and into June. June was heavily scheduled, but I knew I could maintain my fast pace because in July I was going to take my vacation. I had planned to go to northern Italy to visit my relatives. But in early June God revealed that he had other plans for me.

DIAGNOSIS: CANCER

On Saturday, June 3, I noticed that my urine was somewhat discolored, but I did not pay much

attention to it because I thought it might possibly
be related to something I had eaten. But it was like
that on Sunday and again on Monday. That day I
celebrated a late afternoon Mass for the Consuls
General in Chicago at Archbishop Quigley Seminary. After the Mass and reception, I went out for
dinner with my friend Father Scott Donahue.
When we returned to the residence shortly after
10:00 P.M., I casually told him about the discol-
oration. He immediately said, "You'd better call
your doctor." My response must not have convinced him that I was going to make the call, so he
said, "I'm not leaving this house tonight until you
call your doctor."

I called my personal physician, Dr. Warren
Furey, who is chief of staff at Mercy Hospital in
Chicago, and told him what had been occurring.
He scheduled an appointment for me to have a
urine test the next day in his office at Northwestern Memorial Hospital, which is just a block away
from my office at the Pastoral Center of the Archdiocese. He said he would not be there but his
nurse would take care of me.

The next morning, to be honest, I forgot
about my appointment. I thought of it when my

secretary, Sister Ann McCahill, told me that the person who was supposed to meet with me at 11:00 had to cancel his appointment. Only then did I remember the urine test.

I walked over to Northwestern casually and calmly. It was a lovely summer day, and it was good to get out of the office for a few minutes. The nurse greeted me, administered the test, and told me that the office would call with the results. I returned to my office, forgot about the test, and worked until 5:00.

As I was leaving to go home, Sister Ann came running after me and said, "Dr. Furey is on the phone, and he wants to talk to you—it's very important." So I went back to my office, picked up the phone, and said, "Warren, I presume this is the result of the test." "Yes," he said, "we found biliruben in your urine." "Warren," I said jokingly, "who is Billy Ruben and what's he doing in my urine?"

Doctor Furey explained that biliruben often indicates an obstruction and requested that I go to Mercy Hospital for more tests. I told him that the next day, Wednesday, I had to leave the city at 6:00 A.M. for St. Paul, Minnesota, because I had a Mass and homily there for the Catholic Health

Association. "Come in Thursday," he said, "What
kind of a day is that for you?" I told him, "From
9:00 on, it's full." "That's no problem," he said,
"Give me an hour and a half. Come at 7:30 and I'll
have you back in the office by 9:00."

At 7:30 on Thursday morning, my friend
Monsignor Kenneth Velo and I drove to Mercy
Hospital, but I didn't get home until nearly 6:00
that evening! Everything during the day had to be
canceled. I could tell, as could Ken, from the look
on Dr. Furey's face that something was wrong.
They did a CAT scan, as well as blood tests, which
showed that there was some kind of serious block-
age. At that point, though they had fears, they did
not know exactly what it was. Dr. Furey called a
colleague at Northwestern Memorial Hospital
and asked if he could take me immediately for an
ERCP (Endoscopic Retrograde Cholangio Pan-
creatography) test. The answer was yes. We arrived
around 2:00 P.M. I was still smiling and oblivious
to the possibilities when they gave me the anes-
thesia. They inserted a stent (a little hollow tube),
and soon determined that I had a cancerous
tumor. About two hours later I woke up. Standing
there were Dr. Furey, Dr. Robert Craig from

Northwestern, several other attendants, and Ken. I could see that they were rather serious looking, so I asked, "Well, what's the story?"

As I asked the question, a feeling of helplessness came over me. I had regained control of my life after the false accusation and here I was asking somebody else to tell me about *my* life, *my* body. Remembering that moment now, I think of God and his plan for me. I think of others, too, who sit in a state of great anxiety as they wait to hear from doctors what their fate will be. I now realize that when I asked Dr. Furey to tell me the story as reflected in the test results, I had to let go of everything. Again. God was teaching me yet again just how little control we really have and how important it is to trust in him. I needed God at that moment, as I had needed him before.

"You have a tumor in your pancreas," Dr. Furey said. "Oh?" I asked, "What are the possibilities of it being malignant?" Without batting an eye the doctors said, "About 99 percent plus," "I'm in trouble, then," I voiced aloud, only to hear them say, "Yes, you're in a lot of trouble."

We made arrangements for me to go back to Mercy Hospital the next day, Friday. Dr. Furey explained to me the kind of surgery they usually do for this type of cancer if it is discovered in time. Then he investigated what hospitals and doctors were best known for such surgery, assuring me that I would get the best care. After a number of consultations, Dr. Furey informed me that I wouldn't have to go very far for my operation. "The information I have," he said, "is that there is a Dr. Gerard Aranha at Loyola Medical Center in Maywood, Illinois, who is excellent. He's as good as anybody." I felt relieved to know that I would be able to have the surgery so close to home.

Monsignor Velo and I then drove to Loyola. I remember as we neared our destination we saw the big sign that read Loyola University Cancer Center. I had always been afraid of cancer and frequently hesitated even using the word. I asked Ken, "Are you sure we're at the right place?" He said, "Yes, I'm afraid so." So we went in and talked to Dr. Aranha and Dr. Richard Fisher, the head of the Center. They told me that what I needed was the "Whipple" procedure, which I had never heard of before. They explained to me what it was. At that point, Dr. Aranha informed me, "If you're fortunate, it will be a long surgery. If you're not fortunate, it will be very short." I asked when the procedure should be done, and he admonished, "The sooner the better—Monday morning would be the best." I agreed to arrive at the hospital Sunday afternoon to prepare for surgery early Monday morning.

AN ASIDE: MY FATHER

THE MORE I ACCEPTED the terrible reality that I had cancer, the more I thought of my father, Giuseppi (Joseph) Bernardin. He died of cancer in 1934, just seven years after marrying my mother, Maria. I was six and my sister, Elaine, was two. From that day on the three of us lived and worked together to make ends meet. We carried on in his honor the hopes and dreams he brought to America when he and my mother left their hometown of Tonadico di Primiero in Italy to begin life anew in Columbia, South Carolina.

Ever since childhood I have known that cancer changes lives—not only the life of the person carrying it but also the lives of friends and family members who love and care for that person.

Today I often think of my father because he was a brave man who handled his cancer with great dignity. What stands out most vividly are the many times he expressed his love for our family, even in the worst days of his illness.

One memory in particular that I want to share happened when I was four or five. It was summertime, and our family was visiting friends. My father had recently undergone cancer-related surgery on his left shoulder, and he was wearing a bandage under a white short-sleeved shirt. I was sitting on a metal railing on the porch of our friends' home, when suddenly I fell backwards, hit the ground, and started crying. My father immediately jumped over the rail and picked me up. As he held me in his arms, I could see blood soaking through his shirt. He paid no attention to himself; all he wanted was to be sure I was all right.

My father's ability to transcend his own illness and share in the joy of his family and friends now inspires me as I try to do the same. I am grateful to my father for the lessons he taught me when I was young. Today I know that he is alive in me in more ways than I had ever imagined.

SHARING THE NEWS
WITH MY "FAMILY"

AFTER AGREEING TO HAVE THE SURGERY, I told
my doctors, "There's something else that you've
got to do. You have to hold a press conference and
tell the people—my family—exactly what you've
told me." "You're sure you want us to do that?"
they asked. "Yes," I said, "I know you're bound by
confidentiality, but I'm releasing you from that.
There is no way I can undergo this kind of surgery
without telling the people. First of all, I think they
have a right to know, and I have an obligation to
tell them. Besides, I need their prayers. Also, if I
check into this hospital and undergo an eight-
hour operation, goodness knows what the media
will say about it."

That afternoon, June 9, the first press confer-
ence related to my health was held at the Pastoral
Center. Sister Mary Brian Costello, my Chief of
Staff, was recovering from major surgery at Mercy
Hospital, and Bishop Raymond Goedert, our
Vicar General, had to dash back to Chicago from
Belleville, Illinois, where he was giving a priests'

retreat. Bishop Goedert told the media that I had been diagnosed as having pancreatic cancer. Then Dr. Furey explained the medical details and answered questions.

That press conference was only the first of many. The people of metropolitan Chicago and beyond learned more about my insides than they knew about their own! I didn't see that first conference. But I later saw a rerun of it, and it was as though I were living in an unreal world. In a very graphic way I learned that I was carrying a very aggressive type of cancer. Then I learned that my chances of surviving for five years were only one in four or five. I had to make arrangements that weekend before I went into the hospital to turn over responsibility of the Archdiocese to Bishop Goedert. I kept pinching myself, saying, "Is this real? Is this true?" But I was in good spirits. Somehow the Lord gave me the strength I needed.

I called my family, principally my sister, Elaine Addison, who made plans to come to Chicago immediately. All day Saturday and Sunday I got ready for the surgery by making sure that everything regarding the Archdiocese was provided for. About an hour before I left for the hospital Sunday afternoon, Pope John Paul II called and said that he had heard about the surgery and that he wanted me to know that he and his household were praying for me. The Holy Father then spoke about the redemptive value of suffering. I told him that, indeed, I planned to offer whatever suffering there might be for him, for the Church universal, and also for this local church, the priests, and the people of the metropolitan area. After the phone call, Ken Velo and I left the residence and drove to Loyola.

Needless to say, when we arrived there were a lot of media outside the hospital. I gave an impromptu press conference at the entrance. One of the first questions asked was, "Cardinal, which did you find more difficult or more traumatic— the false accusation or the diagnosis of cancer?" I immediately said, "The false accusation." They asked me to explain, so I told them that the accusation had been the result of evil. It was an attack on my integrity, which, had it prevailed, would have ruined my credibility, my ability to lead. But cancer is an illness. It doesn't involve moral evil. It's part of the human condition. And so as serious as it was, it was not nearly so traumatic for me personally as the accusation had been.

SURGERY

WHEN I ENTERED THE HOSPITAL, I went through a battery of tests. Ken and I agreed that we would get up early the next morning to celebrate Mass. He moved in with me—he was in a room across from mine—and made a little makeshift altar. Naturally, I wanted to prepare myself spiritually for what awaited me during the surgery, so it was very important to celebrate the Eucharist that morning and enter into deeper communion with the Lord.

Since I was told they would bring me to the operating room at 6:30 A.M., I planned to celebrate Mass around 5:30. At 6:00 my sister arrived, together with Bishop Goedert and Father Donahue. The mood was quite upbeat. But 6:30 came and went, and nobody came for me. The nurses were checking in, but they didn't come to take me to the operating room. So the tension began to mount as the clocked ticked on. By 7:15 we had all run out of small talk. Ken said, "Excuse me for a couple of minutes." He soon returned with a huge smile on his face and said, "Don't worry, Cardinal, the doctor is on his way. He's running a little late. He was arrested on a DUI charge last night." Well, his humor broke the ice. We all started laughing, and that's how I went to the operating room!

The next thing I knew, I was in the recovery room. As I opened my eyes, Ken was standing there. He paused and said, "Cardinal, it was a long, long surgery." I said, "*Deo gratias*—thanks be to God." Then I went back to sleep.

I spent only one night in the intensive care unit. Then they brought me back to my own room, where I experienced the discomforts one normally encounters after going through extensive surgery. I wanted to pray, but the physical discomfort was overwhelming. I remember saying to the friends who visited me, "Pray while you're well, because if you wait until you're sick you might not be able to do it." They looked at me, astonished. I said, "I'm in so much discomfort that I can't focus on prayer. My faith is still present. There is nothing wrong with my faith, but in terms of prayer, I'm just too preoccupied with the pain. I'm going to remember that I must pray when I am well!"

Since then prayer has been more important to me than ever before. I have savored those moments when my physical pain subsides, and my mind, body, and spirit can focus on the Lord. It is important to remember that prayer is a vital part of our lives as Christians, as believers. But there are so many obstacles to praying with all our hearts and minds. The daily events of life seem to get in the way. And when we are sick, everything changes. I find myself telling priests and parishioners more and more to develop a strong prayer life in their best moments so that they can be sustained in their weaker moments.

AN ASIDE: MY MOTHER

EARLIER I DISCUSSED the connection I now feel with my father, whose manner of dealing with his own cancer has deeply inspired me as I deal with mine. Before I discuss how my cancer ministry began, I want to tell you a little bit about my dear mother, Maria Simion Bernardin, who is almost

92 and lives a short distance from me in the Little Sisters of the Poor Center for the Aging.

Following my father's death, my mother got a job as a seamstress to support Elaine and me. She became both mother and father. Her strength during my childhood and throughout my life has served as a powerful lesson to me. Hard work pays off; love involves dedication and selflessness. These and many other virtues are essential to good family life.

One of my favorite memories from childhood is the hours I spent leafing through the photo album my mother brought with her from Italy. She used to sit down with me and tell the stories of the people and places on each page. Later on I would flip through the album by myself and study all of the details in each photo. When I finally made my first trip to Tonadico with my mother and sister in 1957, I was twenty-nine years old. What surprised me was that I instantaneously felt right at home. Because of the photos I felt as if I had been there before! I have been back to Tonadico many times, and each time I feel at home.

For my mother, teaching Elaine and me about the importance of family was essential. I have always felt blessed to have come from a loving family, and my heart goes out to those who do not share the same experience. I believe, however, as my mother always has, that family goes well beyond blood lines. Family is the human community, the Christian community, and we must learn to love one another as a family. Like any family, we have our disagreements, but in the end we are bonded together.

In the time I was in the hospital recuperating from surgery, and during my subsequent visits for treatment and tests, I have witnessed countless family members and friends caring for a loved one suffering from cancer or other illnesses. I have seen the same resolve on their faces as I had seen on my mother's when she cared for my father, and when she cared for us kids after my father's death. It is tough to watch those we love in pain. But we must believe that by being strong and supportive we make an enormous difference. As I started reaching out to other cancer patients and people with illnesses, I thanked God for all that my mother has taught me through her own strength and kindness.

MY CANCER
MINISTRY BEGINS

ONE OF THE THINGS I HAVE NOTICED most
about illness is that it draws you inside yourself.
When we are ill, we tend to focus on our own pain
and suffering. We may feel sorry for ourselves or
become depressed. But by focusing on Jesus' message—that through suffering we empty ourselves
and are filled with God's grace and love—we can
begin to think of other people and their needs; we
become eager to walk with them in their suffering
and trials.

It was during my recovery and subsequent visits to the hospital for chemotherapy and radiation
that the cancer ministry I've talked about so often
began. I will discuss this special ministry to cancer
patients and others who are ill in more detail later
in this book. Right now I simply want to explain
how it all started.

A day or so after the surgery they had me up
and walking a bit, first in my room and then in the
hallway, with the help of a nurse. I walked with my
IV apparatus on a "tree" with wheels. As I made

my rounds the nurses told me that there was a little girl by the name of Amanda who was being treated for leukemia on another floor. She had been watching all of the television coverage regarding my surgery and told her mother that she wanted to see the "pope man." "I'm not a Catholic," she said, "but he and I both have cancer, and I want to see that pope man." I was not permitted to go off the floor so I sent her a teddy bear and a bouquet of flowers from the many gifts I had been receiving.

Fortunately, I was able to visit with other patients on my floor. I began dropping in to see people, wheeling my entourage of tubes each time.

Immediately next door was a lovely young lady who has since died. She had a very severe form of leukemia and ultimately underwent treatment that required total isolation. She had two beautiful children, a little boy and a little girl. Obviously she wanted to spend as much time with them as possible. When I visited her, the children were sitting in bed with her, one on each side. That was the first of many visits. I kept in touch with them many times after we left the hospital. I also went to the wake when the mother passed away.

Another patient I visited was a young father. He was a handsome man who had just been diagnosed with cancer. I had several good talks with him. It turned out to be a very sad story, however, because I later learned that he committed suicide. He couldn't take it—just the thought of having cancer and making his wife and children go through it with him was too much. I was very saddened when I heard that.

After being released from the hospital, I remained dedicated to visiting people and sharing stories with them. We helped each other. My little friend Amanda still receives chemo on a periodic basis, and when I was at Loyola a few weeks ago for some blood tests, she had left me a beautiful letter in which she invited me to have dinner with her. We've kept up a nice friendship and correspondence. I might add that her penmanship has greatly improved in the past year!

PART THREE

*A Priest First,
a Patient Second*

M E D I T A T I O N

"As Those
Who Serve"

PASTORAL MINISTRY MODELED on that of the Good Shepherd is at once *simple* and *profound*. It is *simple* because it involves people in the routines and emergencies of their daily lives. It can happen at any moment in any place for any reason. It is *profound* because the encounter transcends both minister and flock and brings both into deeper contact with God.

As a *shepherd*, a pastor, Jesus started with real-life situations. He was an itinerant. He had no office, no official hours, no secretary, no computer or fax! He walked the highways and byways of the land, seeking out the lost sheep of Israel. People also flocked to him for a variety of reasons. They wanted to be healed of an illness, to have their questions answered, to have a dispute settled, to be fed with the word of God, or simply to satisfy their curiosity. What is important, however, is that, by caring and being present to them, Jesus enabled the people to experience salvation from God in some way. This is at the very heart of what it means to be a shepherd, a *pastor*: Through authentic ministry people encounter the living God.

Jesus' ministry was not orderly, but we would hardly suggest that it had no focus. He was frequently overextended in ministering to those in need, but he never lost his way. His work, at times, interfered with his sleep, but not with his prayer. For years I wondered how he kept his ministry so clearly on track through all the interruptions and obstacles—all the "mess" of the world that intruded into his life and ministry.

Then one day it struck me that, when Jesus opened his arms to embrace a little child and when he opened his arms wide on the cross to embrace the whole world, it was one and the same. He came to bring the Father's healing, saving love to the human family—one person at a time. He came among us filled with enduring love. So, the people he encountered on his journeys were *never* interruptions, distractions, or obstacles. For him, they were *opportunities* to carry out his mission; this is why the Father had sent him into the world! Serving others was at the very core of the meaning of his life and ministry.

Just before Jesus entered Jerusalem in triumph on Palm Sunday, the mother of James and John asked that he give her sons special positions of honor in his kingdom. Jesus responded: "whoever wants to rank first among you must serve the needs of all. Such is the case with the Son of Man who has come, not to be served by others, but to serve, to give his own life as a ransom for the many" (Mt 20:27–28). Indeed, at the Last Supper on the night before he died, Jesus told his apostles: "Let the great among you be as the junior, the leader as the servant . . . I am in your midst as the one who serves you" (Lk 22:26–27).

At the Last Supper according to the Gospel of John, Jesus also gave his disciples a striking example of service by washing their feet and mandating that they wash each other's feet (Jn 13:1–16). He also gave them a new commandment: "Love one another. Such as my love has been for you, so must your love be for each other. This is how all will know you are my disciples: your love for one another" (Jn 13:34–35). What does this mean, to love as Jesus loves us? He explains later in the Last Discourse: "There is no greater love than this: to lay down one's life for one's friends" (Jn 15:13), as Jesus himself would do the next day.

Service to the people of God in the model of the Good Shepherd is at the very heart of my priestly and episcopal ministry. That is why I chose "As Those Who Serve" as my episcopal motto; it is emblazoned on my coat of arms. It is based on the Second Vatican Council's Decree on the Pastoral Office of Bishops in the Church: "In exercising his office of father and pastor the bishop should be with his people *as one who serves* [italics mine], as a good shepherd who knows his sheep and whose sheep know him, as a true father who excels in his love and solicitude for all."

This service is often quite simple. As Archbishop, when I made parish visitations, I always tried to make people feel at home with me.

Unfortunately, I was not able to stay at any parish for very long. When I took part in parish receptions, however, I tried to look everyone in the eye and make each person feel that he or she was important, the only one present at the moment. This seemed to have an important effect on people. I still receive many very personal letters that begin, "I met you at my home parish several years ago . . ."

Somehow, when you make that eye contact, when you convince people that you really care and that, even if hundreds of others are around, at that particular moment they are the only ones that count—then you establish a new relationship. They leave feeling that they have entered into a special intimacy with you—if only for a moment. They sense that somehow you truly care about them and that, more importantly, you have somehow mediated the love, mercy, and compassion of the Lord. In other words, the encounter also has a significant religious dimension: It helps strengthen the bond, the relationship, between each person and God.

My new ministry to cancer patients has been, then, both simple and profound. It grew out of the ordinary circumstances of my daily life as a cancer patient and drew me closer to the vast community of cancer patients as well as to the Lord of life. At the same time, this new ministry is fully consistent with my life; it is integral to my priesthood. Let me explain what I mean.

HEEDING GOD'S CALL: THE PRIESTHOOD

I N MY SENIOR YEAR OF HIGH SCHOOL, I earned a scholarship to the University of South Carolina. It was quite an honor to be awarded the scholarship, and because money was scarce for my mother, sister, and me, I knew it would be the only way I could get a good education. It was thrilling to think that I would be the first in my family to receive a college education.

I decided to enter the pre-med program. It seemed to me that becoming a doctor would be a noble endeavor, enabling me to help people and at the same time provide the means to live a secure life.

But God had different plans for me.

The summer after my freshman year, I became friends with a couple of young priests from my hometown parish. They took a great interest in me and eventually asked if I had ever thought about entering the priesthood. When I told them that I wanted to become a doctor, they approached the question a different way. They showed me that my interest in becoming a doctor indicated that I wanted to help people, to reach out to others. They proceeded to explain to me that I could also help people by being a priest.

I pondered what these young priests were telling me because I respected them. Almost instantly I decided to enter the seminary. My mother was concerned, of course, that my decision was perhaps too hasty. She also cautioned me that giving up my scholarship could be risky, and that if the seminary did not suit me I would not have anything to fall back on.

I decided to go anyway. God was calling me, and I had to listen.

I studied at Saint Mary's College in Kentucky, Saint Mary's Seminary in Baltimore, and Theological College at the Catholic University of America in Washington, D.C. I was ordained to the priesthood in 1952 for the Diocese of Charleston at Saint Joseph Church, Columbia, South Carolina. During my fourteen years in the Diocese of Charleston, I served many roles under four different bishops. Time and again I found myself smiling to recognize that what those young priests had said about the priesthood was true: through my work I *was* able to help people.

In 1966 I was appointed Auxiliary Bishop of Atlanta by Pope Paul VI. This made me the youngest bishop in the country. Two years later I was elected General Secretary of the National Conference of Catholic Bishops and the United States Catholic Conference and moved to Washington, D.C. During these years my responsibilities and duties continued to grow. I found myself moving farther and farther into administrative work, which, while important to the Church, removed me somewhat from the daily lives and concerns of most people.

In 1972 Pope Paul VI appointed me Archbishop of Cincinnati. I served the Ohio Metropolitan See for almost ten years, during which time I was elected to a three-year term (1974–77) as president of the National Conference of Catholic Bishops and the United States Catholic Conference.

Then in 1982 I was appointed Archbishop of Chicago by Pope John Paul II. Six months later I was elevated to the College of Cardinals.

The past fourteen years in Chicago have been the most productive and blessed years of my life. It is here that I first began to articulate the need for a consistent ethic of life. It is here that I have worked with the nearly 1,800 priests who help shepherd the 2.3 million Catholics in the archdiocese, which covers 1,411 square miles of Lake and Cook counties, includes 48 high schools, 281 elementary schools, 6 colleges or universities, 19 hospitals, and 3 archdiocesan seminaries.

As a priest, I am called to be an instrument of God's will, of his intimate love for and relationship to all living persons. Throughout my ministry I have known this. The basic definition or the basic qualities of the priesthood don't change. And because I live by them, many people tell me that I'm the same now as I was forty years ago. I was more naive in those early days—the world had not changed as much as it has since then. Everything was pretty uniform in the Church before the Second Vatican Council. And in one sense, we priests were more familiar with our role, or at least with what people expected of us.

But even with all of the changes that have taken place since the 1960s, most people who know me well would agree that I have not really changed. I have always cared for people. I have always tried to reconcile people. I have always tried to be the instrument of God's healing love.

Yet, I have never understood what it means to be a priest more clearly than I do now. People look to priests to be authentic witnesses to God's active role in the world, to his love. They don't want us to be politicians or business managers; they are not interested in the petty conflicts that may show up in parish or diocesan life. Instead, people simply want us to be with them in the joys and sorrows of their lives. I understand that organization is important. The Church as a human institution needs a certain amount of administration. But structures can take on a life of their own and obscure the real work with people that priests should be doing.

I have never felt more like a priest than I have in the past year. Following my first round of chemotherapy and radiation treatments, I told my advisers that I now had a new priority in my ministry: spending time with the sick and the troubled. No matter how significant our other work might be, the people want something different from their clergy. Even if they are not committed to any specific religion, men and women everywhere have a deep desire to come into contact with the transcendent. Members of the clergy can facilitate this through the simple goodness they show in being with their people. The things people are naturally attracted to and remember most are small acts of concern and thoughtfulness. Years later, *that* is what they tell you about their priests and other clergy.

"UNOFFICIAL CHAPLAIN" TO CANCER PATIENTS

WHAT BEGAN AS VISITS to other patients who shared the same floor with me at Loyola Medical Center has since blossomed into a wonderful and life-giving ministry.

When I was released from the hospital on Monday, June 19, 1995, I carried in my heart all those I had met at Loyola. That day was emotional in so many ways, especially because of all the love and support I received from people in Chicago and all over the world. As usual, the media were outside the hospital waiting for me to come out. I wanted to walk out on my own, but the hospital has a rule that anyone who has had surgery must go to the door in a wheelchair. Most of the photos of me that day show me in my wheelchair, even though I did get up and walk once we reached the doors. I must say that I was not as strong that Monday as I had been the week before, but I was doing pretty well.

My postoperative cancer treatment did not begin until July 10, which gave me three weeks to regain my strength. It was very meaningful to me that I began treatment on July 10 because that was the day I had been appointed as Archbishop of Chicago thirteen years earlier. That was a day of confidence and hope, certainly for me, and I trust for the people of the Archdiocese. So, I began the cancer treatment with the same spirit of confidence and hope.

During my time off I began to do something I have always enjoyed: I walked around the neighborhood. At first I would go only a block or two. Eventually I resumed my old route from my residence to the Chicago River and back—about 2.5 miles. But that did not happen all at once; I moved slowly and carefully.

All the while I was preparing for my upcoming treatments, letters, faxes, and phone calls of support and encouragement came pouring in.

Cancer patients and others suffering from serious diseases let me know they were praying for me, and they asked that I pray for them.

Soon I was making phone calls and writing letters to people whose names I had gotten from friends and others who looked to me for advice and spiritual guidance. It wasn't long before the media picked up on my ministry and publicized what I was doing. Then my cancer ministry really grew! I recognized with a sense of humility that I'd quietly become the "unofficial chaplain" to cancer patients. It meant a great deal to me that people felt they could come to me. And I found myself time and again being inspired by the bravery and deep faith of others who shared similar battles with cancer.

A SPECIAL COMMUNITY

THROUGHOUT MY PRIESTHOOD, I have always taken seriously my role as one who reaches out to others with compassion and understanding, as one who bears witness to the faith. But I am fully a part of the human community; I am a brother. And because I am a servant of God, I feel much freer to enter into many different communities, each with its own special defining characteristics, and to emphasize solidarity with the much larger human community.

In the light of my cancer ministry, I began to recognize the unique and special nature of another community to which I now belong: the community of those who suffer from cancer and other serious illnesses. Those in this community see things differently. Life takes on new meaning, and suddenly it becomes easier to separate the essential from the peripheral.

As with any community, it is important to share our personal stories, to connect with people, to be understood.

Time and again I have stood in awe as people suffering from life-threatening illnesses have shared with me their insights into life. I have been inspired to see how truly human and how truly wise they are. So often in the past I, like most of us, have struggled with what to say to people who are suffering. But since I was diagnosed as having cancer, words have come much more easily. So has the ability to know when to listen or to simply reach out my hand.

Throughout my own illness I have shared the news about my health as it has been made known to me. My family are the people of metropolitan Chicago—and also of this country and the world. And my family has a right to know how I am doing.

People have told me many times that I am courageous. My decision to discuss my cancer openly and honestly has sent a message that when we are ill, we need not close in on ourselves or remove ourselves from others. Instead, it is during these times when we need people the most.

Some of the media and individuals have also called me a holy man. I do not, however, feel comfortable with this. I have tried to live my life openly and honestly with a deep commitment to the Lord, the Church, and the human community. The past three years have challenged me like never before to hold firm to my beliefs and to trust in the Lord. But my main point has been to put my faith into action, to live out the principles that guide my life. Above all else, I want people to know that I walk with them as their brother, their friend.

My decision to go through my cancer in public has been to share a simple message: faith really matters. By being grounded in the Lord, by opening

myself to his will, I have been able to accept my illness—and now my impending death. What people
have seen in the papers or on television has not been
a man who wants to look brave or courageous.
What they see is a man who believes in God and
whose faith informs everything he does. Suffering
and pain make little sense to me without God, and
my heart goes out to people who feel abandoned or
alone in their greatest times of need. As a man of
faith, I can really speak of pain and suffering only in
terms of their redemptive, salvific qualities. This
does not mean I have not prayed, as Jesus did, that
it might be God's will that "this cup pass me by."
But by embracing the pain, by looking into it and
beyond it, I have come to see God's presence in
even the worst situations.

PRACTICING WHAT I PREACH

JUST PRIOR TO MY SURGERY, many people asked
me to share my thoughts. I said, "I've been a priest
for 43 years and a bishop for 29 of those years. I
have always told others to put themselves in the
hands of the Lord. I've counseled many people

who faced what I am facing. Now it is time for me
to practice what I preach."

During that time I prayed to God for the grace
to handle my surgery and postoperative treatment
faithfully, without bitterness or undue anxiety.
God's special gift to me has been the ability to
accept difficult situations, especially the false
accusation made against me and then the cancer.
His special gift to me is the gift of peace.

In turn, my special gift to others is to share
God's peace, to help them deal with illness, troubled times.

By talking about my inner peace, I hope people can see that there is a lot more to prayer and
faith than mere words. God really does help us live
fully even in the worst of times. And the capacity
to do precisely this depends upon the deepening of
our relationship to God through prayer.

AN ASIDE:
THE IMPORTANCE OF PRAYER

I LEARNED MANY YEARS AGO that the only way I
could give quality time to prayer was by getting up

early in the morning. (I must add parenthetically that I didn't have a great desire to get up so early—I usually tried to stay in bed as late as I could.) The early hours of the morning, before the phones and doorbells started to ring, before the mail arrived, seemed to me to be the best for spending quality time with the Lord. So I promised God and myself that I would give the first hour of each day to prayer. Though not knowing then whether I would keep this promise, I'm happy to say that I have kept it for nearly twenty years. This doesn't mean that I've learned how to pray perfectly. It doesn't mean that I have not experienced the struggles that other people have faced. Quite the contrary. But early on, I made another decision. I said, "Lord, I know that I spend a certain amount of that morning hour of prayer daydreaming, problem-solving, and I'm not sure that I can cut that out. I'll try, but the important thing is, I'm not going to give that time to anybody else. So even though it may not unite me as much with you as it should, nobody else is going to get that time."

What I have found as time has gone on is that the effect of that first hour doesn't end when the hour is up. That hour certainly unites me with the

Lord in the early part of the day, but it keeps me connected to him throughout the rest of the day as well. Frequently as I face issues, whether positive or negative, I think of my relationship to the Lord and ask for his help. So these are two important points, at least for me. Namely, even if it's not used right, you shouldn't give that time to somebody else; you should just keep plugging away. And secondly, if you do give the time, little by little you become united with the Lord throughout your life, which is very important.

What do I do during my morning prayer? I pray some of the Liturgy of the Hours. For me, that's a very important prayer. It's a prayer of the Church, and I feel connected with all the people, especially clerics and religious, who are reciting or praying the Liturgy of the Hours throughout the world. And so it gives me not only the feeling but also the conviction that I'm part of something that is much greater. And secondly, a major portion of the prayers of the various hours are from the Psalms. I have found the Psalms to be very special because they relate in a very direct, human way the joys and sorrows of life, the virtues, the sins. They convey the message that good ultimately wins out. And as you see the people who are mentioned in the Psalms struggling to be united with the Lord, it gives you a certain amount of encouragement, knowing that even thousands of years ago this same thing was happening.

I also pray the Rosary because it brings into vivid images some of the high points in the Lord's life and ministry as well as that of his Blessed Mother. It's a real help. Some people think it may be repetitious, and in a sense it is. But it keeps you focused on the mysteries of the Lord, Joyful Mysteries, Sorrowful Mysteries, Glorious Mysteries.

And then I spend part of my time in mental prayer, reflection. I try to enrich that as much as I can by prayerfully reflecting on the Scriptures and other good spiritual books. As I have said, I was a bit taken aback when I realized that during the period of my convalescence, immediately after the surgery, I really didn't have the desire or the strength to pray. And that's when I said to some friends, "Make sure that you pray when you're well because when you're real sick, you probably won't." But that in no way undermined my faith in the Lord. I have found this to be very valuable for

some of my fellow cancer patients. They sometimes think that their faith is waning when they
are not able to pray as intensely as they might have
before. But I go back to one word: *connected.*
Without prayer, you cannot be connected or
you cannot remain united with the Lord. It's
absolutely essential.

A PRIEST FIRST,
AND A PATIENT SECOND

BEFORE I WAS RELEASED from the hospital on
June 19, 1995, I was introduced to Dr. Anne R.
McCall, my radiologist, and to Dr. Ellen Gaynor,
who has been my oncologist and dear friend
ever since.

They explained to me that once my postoperative treatment began on July 10, I would receive
daily radiation treatments for about six weeks,
with weekends off. During the same time, I would
undergo chemotherapy injections every two weeks
to boost the effectiveness of the radiation. The
doctors explained to me that I might experience
side effects such as fatigue and digestive problems,

but that I would not experience any visible side effects, such as hair loss. I joked with them that I really didn't have much hair left to lose, at which they smiled and said I shouldn't have anything to worry about.

My treatment sessions took only about ten minutes, but my visits to the hospital lasted as long as five hours. I would take the opportunity to check in on people, to pray with them and their loved ones. One day one of the doctors told me, "Cardinal, if you wish, you can come into the area through the back door so you can come and go quietly." I paused a moment and answered, "I'm a priest first, a patient second."

One of the stories that came from my visits has found its way into many of my homilies and speeches in recent months. It is worth sharing here.

During my radiation treatments I met a woman named Lottie, who was undergoing the same treatment I was. She was quite ill, and I was not sure how much longer she was going to live. We finished our treatments about the same time in early August. During that month I stayed in touch with her and could tell that she was worsening. And finally, on the day before Labor Day, her daughter, Chris, called and said, "Cardinal, my mother is sinking very, very fast. I don't think she can live much longer." I immediately said that I would visit Lottie, who, along with her husband, was staying with her daughter.

When I arrived, Chris said, "My mother is very fitful, full of anxiety, she's only semiconscious." I went in to talk with Lottie. I don't know whether she really recognized me, but I spoke to her and anointed her. Then when I came out of the room, Chris said, "You know, I think one of the problems is that my father keeps going in there and telling her, 'Lottie, you can't go, I need you, you can't die.'" She then asked me, "Would you talk to my father?"

I spoke with Lottie's husband and suggested to him that maybe the time had come to let his wife go. Chris called me that night to tell me that only a few minutes after I left she saw her father go into the bedroom and then heard him say, "Lottie, it's okay for you to go now." Chris said that her mother immediately became tranquil, and two days later she died peacefully.

FURTHER CHALLENGES

AFTER I BEGAN TREATMENT, complications arose that were to give me a lot of trouble later on. As I was walking with Father Velo, I would say, "Ken, my legs feel funny." "How do they feel?" he asked. "Well," I said, "You know when you have a fever, you feel as though your arms and legs don't belong to you; that's how my legs feel. It must be the radiation or the chemo."

So I asked my doctors at Loyola, "Is the problem with my legs a side effect of the radiation or the chemo?" "No," they said, "you shouldn't have any difficulty with your legs." But my legs kept getting worse.

In November 1995 I had the first of several falls as a result of the weakness in my legs. I was at the Villa in Mundelein when I fell and fractured a vertebra. Then in late January, I fell on the stairs of my residence. Over the next six to eight months I fractured four vertebrae in all and four ribs, which caused a great deal of pain. Doctors soon discovered that in addition to having spinal stenosis, I had osteoporosis as well as a curvature of the spine. I lost four inches in height! Consequently, I had to have my cardinalatial robes shortened.

Despite the constant pain in my back and legs, in late summer 1995 I was getting along very well with the cancer treatment, and my morale was excellent.

One of my favorite memories of this time was hosting the grand finale of "Theology-on-Tap," a four-week lecture series designed for the Archdiocese of Chicago and the Diocese of Joliet's twenty- and thirty-somethings. The program has been in existence for fourteen years, and each year thousands of young people come together to listen to speakers and explore with one another the many dimensions of their faith. At the end of the four weeks, everyone gathers on the lawn of my residence for food, beverages, music, and fun. Although I always look forward to sharing in the excitement, I didn't think that I'd be able to make it that year.

But I did! And everyone greeted me with such love and encouragement that I couldn't stop smiling. One man yelled out, "I hope you feel as good as you look!" Ordinarily I would be honest and say that I didn't. On that day, however, I really felt good through and through.

When the radiation and chemotherapy ended in mid-August, I had another month off.

Then in mid-September I began a "maintenance program," which consisted of a weekly injection of chemotherapy called 5FU—(5-fluorouracil), a chemical used to fight off pancreatic cancer. The aftereffects of those injections (which I received at home) were quite tolerable. The injections were supposed to continue for two years.

"A SIGN OF HOPE": MY PASTORAL LETTER ON HEALTHCARE

CONFRONTING MY OWN CANCER and sharing time with other cancer patients have deepened my commitment to arguing the case for maintaining quality healthcare that is accessible to everyone who needs it. When I was released from Loyola University Medical Center on June 19, 1995, I paid my doctors the highest compliment I think a patient can say to a healthcare provider. I told them that what impressed me most about their staff was that they treated all the patients with equal respect and compassion. I expected to be treated well, but I soon realized that everybody was treated the same. Skin color, race, gender, and socioeconomic status did not matter. I told the doctors and medical staff that they should be proud of the wonderful treatment they give.

In October 1995 I released a pastoral letter on healthcare called "A Sign of Hope." It had been four months since my surgery, and healthcare was very much on my mind. I decided to begin the document with a very personal letter that I believe is worth sharing here.

During my entire ministry as a bishop, especially during the past two years, I have invested considerable time and energy on issues related to Catholic healthcare. When healthcare reform became part of the public policy debate last year, I made several contributions to that discussion— pointing out, for example, the importance of the not-for-profit status of Catholic healthcare institutions. In all of my efforts I have expressed my appreciation for the past and current dedication to, and service in, the ministry of Catholic healthcare by the religious women and men who sponsor this ministry and the dedicated laymen and women who collaborate with them.

Several months ago, I decided to write this pastoral reflection on Catholic healthcare to bring together several of my concerns and to give some direction to healthcare ministry in the Archdiocese of Chicago. However, before I was able to begin the project, I was diagnosed with pancreatic cancer. After surgery at Loyola University Medical Center in Maywood, Illinois, and a brief period of recuperation, I underwent nearly six weeks of radiation therapy and chemotherapy.

Now I return to this project not only as a bishop with an abiding interest in, and commitment to, Catholic healthcare, but also as a cancer patient who has benefited greatly from this competent, compassionate care in the model of Jesus the healer.

When I entered the Loyola University Medical Center last June, my life had been turned completely upside down by the totally unexpected news that what I had been experiencing as a healthy body was, in fact, housing a dangerous, aggressive cancer. The time since the diagnosis, surgery, and postoperative radiation and chemotherapy has led me into a new dimension of my life-long journey of faith.

I have experienced in a very personal way the chaos that serious illness brings into one's life. I have had to let go of many things that had brought me a sense of security and satisfaction in order to find the healing that only faith in the Lord can bring.

Initially, I felt as though floodwaters were threatening to overwhelm me. For the first time in my life I truly had to look death in the face. In one brief moment, all my personal dreams and pastoral plans for the future had to be put on hold. Everything in my personal life and pastoral ministry had to be re-evaluated from a new perspective. My initial experience was of disorientation, isolation, a feeling of not being "at home" anymore.

Instead of being immobilized by the news of the cancer, however, I began to prepare myself for surgery and postoperative care. I discussed my condition with family and friends. I prayed as I have never prayed before that I would have the courage and grace to face whatever lay ahead. I determined that I would offer whatever suffering I might endure for the Church, particularly the Archdiocese of Chicago. Blessedly, a peace of mind and heart and soul quietly flooded through my entire being, a kind of peace I had never known before. And I came to believe in a new way that the Lord would walk with me through this journey of illness that would take me from a former way of life into a new manner of living.

Nevertheless, during my convalescence I found the nights to be especially long, a time for various fears to surface. I sometimes found myself weeping, something I seldom did before. And I came to realize how much of what consumes our daily life is trivial and insignificant. In these dark moments, besides my faith and trust in the Lord, I was constantly bolstered by the awareness that thousands of people were

praying for me throughout the Archdiocese and, indeed, the world. I have been
graced by an outpouring of affection and
support that has allowed me to experience
ecclesial life as a "community of hope" in a
very intimate way.

I have also felt a special solidarity with
others facing life-threatening illness. I
have talked and prayed with other cancer
patients who were waiting in the same
room for radiation or chemotherapy. I have
been contacted by hundreds of people
seeking my advice and prayers on behalf of
family or friends suffering a serious illness,
often cancer.

This experience of the past four months
plays an important role in shaping this pastoral reflection on Catholic healthcare. I
have reason to believe that my reflections on
my illness as well as on the state and future
of Catholic healthcare will help and interest
others who are struggling either with illness
itself or with the delivery of healthcare ser-
vices in a rapidly changing social, economic,
and political environment.

LETTERS FROM
FELLOW CANCER PATIENTS

As I HAVE COME INTO CONTACT with people who are ill or are praying for friends and relatives who are ill, I have compiled a prayer list of their names. At first my prayer list was small enough so that I could recite all the names during my daily Mass. As it has grown, however, I am no longer able to say the names one by one. The list contains more than 700 now! What I do is to hold in my hands the prayer list as I pray to God for all who suffer from cancer and other serious illnesses.

Many of the letters I have received are dear to my heart. These letters say more about my ministry than I ever could. I would like to share some of them with you.

July 31, 1996

Dear Cardinal Bernardin,

Hi, I'm Irene Compra. I'm eight years old. I'm a student at St. Matthew's School, and I'm going into 3rd grade.

Please pray for my aunt, she has cancer,
and also for my uncle, he has cancer too.

Thank you,

Irene

August 6, 1996

Dear Cardinal Bernardin,

My grandmother, Marion Spencer, had
the pleasure of sitting next to you at a
luncheon last year. She spoke of her conversation with you and beamed with
sunshine for weeks. Her faith in God and
her love of her family are two of the defining factors in and of her life.

This past Saturday, as we were leaving
our annual family picnic, grandmother had
a stroke. She is at Palos Community
Hospital, in Palos Hills. If in your busy
schedule you are near there I am sure it
would do her well to see you again.

Thank you,

Joe Spencer

Dear Cardinal Bernardin,

Nine months ago I wrote to you asking you to pray for my seven-year-old son who has cancer. I wanted to again thank you for your prayers and tell you that he continues to do very well. He is a very happy and active boy.

It has now been over a year since the malignant lymph nodes were removed from him and so far there is no sign of cancer. We continue to pray that it never returns.

Also our family prays for you daily. We feel very confident that our prayers have been answered.

Sincerely,
Teri Ellis

September 13, 1996

Your Eminence,

You must be inundated with prayer requests for particular intentions. Mine is no different.

My wife, Ann, who is forty-four, was operated on for colon cancer on December 8, 1995, at Loyola. She's completed a six-month protocol involving continuous chemo infusion and the prognosis is guardedly good. She is the mother of six, ages four to sixteen. She is also the primary nurse and caregiver to our thirteen-year-old son, Martin, who sustained a massive head trauma ten years ago which left him completely dependent. She is in all ways a loving, nurturing wife and mother that I've been blessed to be married to these past seventeen years. I beg your prayers on her and Martin's behalf.

I've followed with many others your trials over the years, both personal and pastoral. It is my admiration of and respect for the Faith-filled way with which you've dealt with these that emboldens me to seek your intercession with the Lord.

As a farmer, I pay attention to the seasons, out of necessity as well as privilege. I know, Cardinal Bernardin, that your harvest season is near. May God grant you the courage born of Faith to, as St. Therese says, "see our life of time for what it is: A passage to eternity."

I thank you for your precious time.

Respectfully,

James Hermes

∾

September 18, 1996

Dear Rev. Father,

In June of this year, I learned that I have prostate cancer. Thus began an exhaustive trek through mounds of research and from doctor to doctor, as I tried to decide what to do about it.

During the months that followed, my fears and anxieties grew, as my wife and I swayed in favor of one treatment, then another. On August 31st, the day after your sad announcement about your terminal cancer, my wife and I attended the service you held at St. Barbara's for the anointing of the sick.

I felt a special kinship with you as we listened to you speak about your feelings in the months immediately following your initial diagnosis of pancreatic cancer. I was touched as you spoke so eloquently of the peace you now hold in your heart and I said to my wife, "I really want Cardinal Bernardin to bless me."

Somehow, I found my way to the center aisle and was instructed to move to one of the shorter lines. I was quickly administered to by a priest who laid his hands upon my head. But instead of continuing forward in the same line, I stood next to you, as you finished blessing another supplicant. Then you looked at me as if to say, "Where did you come from?"

"Forgive me father," I said "I was recently diagnosed with prostate cancer, and I came here today, hoping you might anoint me."

You paused briefly, smiled and said, "And so I shall."

I have drifted away from my Catholic upbringing and can't say I will return to the Church. But I wanted you to know that when you touched my palm with the holy oil, then squeezed my hand affectionately and said, "I will pray for you," a great sense of inner peace swept over me.

I am still scared stiff about what lies ahead. Tomorrow, my wife and I leave for the Mayo Clinic in Scottsdale where I will be evaluated for a somewhat controversial procedure involving the placement of radioactive "seeds" in the prostate. As I take this step, you continue to be a source of great inspiration to me, not just because of the incredible dignity with which you are facing your disease, but because of the compassion, humility, and grace you have consistently demonstrated throughout your life.

I shall pray for you, too, as you face what you have said is your life's greatest challenge.

May God be with you on your journey.
Jack McGuire

September 20, 1996

Dear Cardinal Bernardin,

It is probably bold of me to contact you at all, but we wanted you to know how you have touched our lives.

In early May of this year my fifty-seven-year-old husband was told he had been misdiagnosed. The back pain was not from thirty-six years of truck driving sixty to eighty hours per week, but pancreatic and bile duct cancer. Truthfully, Rex was and is very frightened and full of fear.

In more or less a state of shock, I went to my perpetual adoration hour and picked up the *Liguorian* article discussing your cancer. The next morning I mentioned the article to my brother, Pat. He made a series of phone calls, starting with the Archdiocese of Cincinnati and ending up with the secretary of your surgeon. Your doctor returned my brother's calls that evening. We were very surprised at that. He suggested we call Dr. Josef E. Fischer at University Hospital in Cincinnati. We got an impossible-to-get appointment and after some puzzlement and wondering who the heck we were, Dr. Fischer rearranged his schedule to do extensive surgery on Rex.

What we wanted you to know was that through all the time in the hospital, chemotherapy treatments, and emergency room visits, our buzz words to Rex were "Remember Rex, you know Joe." I had read in that article that all your friends call you Joe and we counted you as our friend without ever meeting you.

Rex's prognosis is poor and he is weak. He has lost a lot of weight and is still scared. We are just taking it a day at a time. The doctors have said that his number is up, but my husband of thirty-six years says that they are not in charge of numbers.

Please pray for us. Thanks for being "our friend Joe." I remember you in my daily prayers especially to St. Peregrine and St. Michael of the Saints.

With love and respect,
Rex and Emily Weeks

PART FOUR

Befriending Death

MEDITATION

"Come to Me All you Who Are Weary and Find Life Burdensome"

ON AUGUST 31, 1996, the day after I announced that the cancer had spread to my liver and was inoperable, I presided at a communal anointing of the sick at Saint Barbara Church in Brookfield, Illinois. I told my fellow sick that, when we are faced with serious illness (or any serious difficulty), we should do several things—things that have given me peace of mind personally.

The first is to put ourselves *completely* in the hands of the Lord. We must believe that the Lord loves us, embraces us, never abandons us (especially in our most difficult moments). This is what gives us hope in the midst of life's suffering and chaos. It is the same Lord who invites us: "Come to me all you who are weary and find life burdensome, and I will refresh you. Take my yoke upon your shoulders and learn from me, for I am gentle and humble of heart. Your souls will find rest, for my yoke is easy and my burden light" (Mt 11:28–30).

This is a favorite passage of mine and, possibly, one of yours also. It is so comforting, so soothing. Perhaps it also sounds too good to be true. Indeed, further reflection shows that Jesus' message is a bit more complex than it appears at first sight or hearing.

For example, is there not a tension between the "rest" that Jesus offers and the "yoke" he invites us to wear? What did Jesus mean by his "yoke"? The ancient rabbis used to refer to the Mosaic Law as a kind of yoke. But Jesus' metaphor is different because central to his "yoke" or wisdom or law is the Lord himself. He practiced what he preached. He was gentle toward the people he served and humbly obedient to the will of his Father. He called us to love one another and laid down his own life for us. The "rest" he offers us comes from adopting and living each day his attitudes, his values, his mission, his ministry, his willingness to lay down his very life—in whatever circumstances we find ourselves.

What makes Jesus' yoke "easy"? A good yoke is carefully shaped to reduce chafing to a minimum. Jesus promises that his yoke will be kind and gentle to our shoulders, enabling us to carry our load more easily. That is what he means when he says his burden is "light." Actually, it might be quite heavy, but we will find it possible to carry out our responsibilities. Why? Because Jesus will help us. Usually a yoke joined a pair of oxen and made them a team. It is as though Jesus tells us, "Walk alongside me; learn to carry the burdens by observing how I do it. If you let me help you, the heavy labor will seem lighter."

Perhaps, the ultimate burden is death itself. It is often preceded by pain and suffering, sometimes extreme hardships. In my case it is primarily a question of a pervasive fatigue that seems to increase day by day, forcing me to spend much of the day and night lying down. But notice that Jesus did not promise to take away our burdens. He promised to help us carry them. And if we let go of ourselves—and our own resources—and allow the Lord to help us, we will be able to see death not as an enemy or a threat but as a friend.

A VISIT FROM
AN OLD FRIEND

A VERY SIGNIFICANT THING happened during the month of July last year. Father Henri Nouwen, a friend of mine for more than twenty-five years, paid me a visit. He had come to a conference in the metropolitan area and asked if he could come to see me. I said, "By all means." We spent over an hour together, and he brought me one of his latest books, *Our Greatest Gift: A Reflection on Dying and Caring*. We talked about the book, and the main thing I remember is that he talked about the importance of looking on death as a friend rather than an enemy. While I had always taken such a view in terms of my faith, I needed to be reminded at that moment because I was rather exhausted from the radiation treatments. "It's very simple," he said. "If you have fear and anxiety and you talk to a friend, then those fears and anxieties are minimized and could even disappear. If you see them as an enemy, then you go into a state of denial and try to get as far away as possible from them." He said, "People of faith, who believe that death is the transition from this life to life eternal, should see it as a friend."

This conversation was a great help to me. It removed some of my anxiety or fear about death for myself. When Father Nouwen died suddenly of a heart attack on September 21 of this year at the age of 59, everyone was shocked. Yet, there is no doubt that he was prepared. He spent a lifetime teaching others how to live, and how to die.

THE CANCER RETURNS

ABOVE MY BED for the last twenty-four years has hung a beautiful carved ivory crucifix mounted on a wooden background. It has been a constant reminder of Jesus' death and resurrection. But when I first wake up in the morning, I usually do not see the crucifix. It is above the head of the bed, so I have to make a deliberate effort to look up at it.

The shadow of the cross falls upon each of our lives, although we are not usually aware of it each day. This is how it was for me until late August of this year. Since then the cross has become my constant companion, a reminder of my upcoming encounter with my new friend, death, who will lead me home to God.

As August 1996 began, I kept a rather full schedule despite the constant pain in my back and legs. When my friends asked whether I should be so active, I told them that my back hurt whether I was sitting, standing, or walking. The pain was no different in Chicago or Washington or Rome. Sometimes I joked that a bishop needs a good head and a good heart, but not necessarily a good back. On August 5, our Office of Communications issued a statement noting that I remained cancer-free and was preparing for spinal surgery that had been scheduled for mid-September. My doctors told me that the best preparation for the surgery would be a normal schedule and as much rest as possible. I met with the surgeon who told me that the surgery would almost surely eliminate most, if not all, of the pain I had experienced for more than nine months.

During the first days of August, I prepared for an August 12 press conference in which I announced the establishment of the Catholic Common Ground Project, an endeavor that had been in the making for more than two years. As head of the initiative, I looked forward to this important forum for helping Catholics to address, creatively and faithfully, questions that are vital if the Church in the United States is to flourish as we enter the next millennium. I felt that, at every level, we needed to move beyond the distrust, the polarization, and the entrenched positions that have hampered our responses.

For the most part, there was an immediate, heartwarming response to the announcement of the initiative. An outpouring of personal letters was sent to me and to the National Pastoral Life Center in New York, which provides the staff for the project. Both priests and parishioners offered support and ideas. A few apparently viewed the Project as another arena for doing battle, while some others feared that it would lead to compromise on matters of Church teaching. I prepared a response in question-and-answer format, in part to reassure people that the Catholic Common Ground Project would be carried on within the boundaries of authentic Church teaching.

On Tuesday, August 27, I met with my Cabinet from the Archdiocese and told them in my monthly report that I had had a full series of blood tests the previous week. The tests revealed there was no sign of cancer. I also told the Cabinet that I was going to the Loyola Medical Center the next day for an MRI (Magnetic Resonance Imaging), a last checkup to be sure that I would be able to undergo spinal surgery on September 16.

I also told the Cabinet about a communal anointing of the sick over which I had presided at Saint John Brébeuf Church in Niles, Illinois, the previous Saturday. It was the first of three such anointings already on my schedule as part of my ministry to cancer patients and others with serious illness. The Cabinet and I discussed the possibility of adding a fourth service at Saint Agatha's Church in the near future. I told them what a moving experience it was as the sick, the elderly, and the dying came forward for the laying on of hands and anointing with the oil of the sick. As a cancer patient, I, too, had been anointed. Receiving this sacrament in the company of so many members of this local church was a moving experience for me and for them.

At the same time I had been cancer-free for fifteen months since the initial diagnosis and surgery for pancreatic cancer. I accepted the odds that the doctors gave me so directly at the time: I had one chance in four of living for five years. The results of regular follow-up examinations were consistently negative. As I mentioned above, even the blood tests taken some days earlier affirmed my sense that I was holding my own. So, on Wednesday, August 28, I went to Loyola for the MRI with confidence.

But after the MRI the somber face of my wonderful oncologist, Dr. Ellen Gaynor, immediately told me that something was wrong.

"We'll have to talk about this," she said. Before, she had always said, "Cardinal, everything is fine!" A few minutes later she told me that there were five cancerous tumors in my liver, one of them two inches in diameter. I had not expected this news at all. Although Dr. Gaynor had repeatedly told me that it was too soon to think I had beaten the odds, I couldn't suppress my hopeful enthusiasm. But on that day I learned that I had, indeed, been carrying the deadly seeds of the cancer's return during the months of hope when I thought I was getting better.

Dr. Gaynor told me that I had only a year or less to live. I immediately identified with Jesus in the Garden of Gethsemane. At that moment—on the eve of the suffering and death that would complete the mission his Father had given to him—Jesus was very lonely, as was I.

That moment, however, passed rather quickly. Quite simply, I am grounded in the Lord and realized that I had been asked to enter more deeply into the mystery of his death and resurrection. I am also grounded in his Church to which I have dedicated my life and ministry for more than four decades and in which, in good times and bad, I have been buoyed by the loving support of its bishops, priests, deacons, religious, and lay faithful. Jesus' words, recorded in the Saint John's Gospel, quickly became my own: "I will not leave you orphans" (Jn 14:18). With God's strength, I said to myself, I will be their pastor as long as possible.

Still, it took me some time to grasp the significance of what Dr. Gaynor had told me. The next day I met in the morning with my senior administrative team—Bishop Raymond Goedert, Father Peter Bowman, Sister Mary Brian Costello, and Brother Dennis Dunne—to inform them about the cancer's return and the fact that it was inoperable. I also explained that the spinal surgery had been canceled because such an operation is usually done only when the prospects for life are more promising. Moreover, if the surgery took place, it would delay the different kind of chemotherapy that Dr. Gaynor had recommended. I then went to my office at the Pastoral Center to sign some letters, talk with some of my immediate staff, and begin to prepare for a press conference the next day.

DYING PUBLICLY

ON FRIDAY, AUGUST 30, I met with the media. The room was so crowded with reporters and TV cameras that it was difficult to move. I shared the news about the latest diagnosis and the estimate that my life expectancy was one year or less. "I have been assured that I still have some quality time left," I said. "My prayer is that I will use whatever time is left in a positive way, that is, in a way that will be of benefit to the priests and people I have been called to serve, as well as to my own spiritual well-being."

I added that, over the past year, I had counseled the cancer patients with whom I had been in contact to place themselves entirely in the hands of the Lord. "I have personally always tried to do that; now I have done so with greater conviction and trust than ever before. While I know that, humanly speaking, I will have to deal with difficult moments, I can say in all sincerity that I am at peace. I consider this as God's special gift to me at this moment in my life."

I also shared with the reporters and my friends and associates who were present what I had learned from Father Nouwen—to look upon death as a friend, not an enemy. I told them that I would continue to serve the Archdiocese in the way I had in the past, keeping a full schedule for as long as I could.

I then spoke directly to the priests and people of the Archdiocese: "Pray that I may continue to serve you and the broader Church with understanding, compassion, and fidelity. Through our solidarity and mutual support and trust, may we give a credible witness to God's love for all of us."

During my entire tenure as Archbishop of Chicago and especially during the past three years, I had been in contact with the media a great deal. So I added a few words to them: "We have enjoyed a good professional relationship in

the years I have been Archbishop of Chicago—
and this will continue. Now I ask that you stand
with me personally. Whatever your religious
affiliation may be, I ask that you say a prayer for
me. And, in return, I will pray for you and your
loved ones."

In the questions that followed my statement, a
reporter asked me if I had anything special I
wanted to accomplish during the time I had left.
Frankly, I had not had a great deal of time to
reflect on that since learning that my disease was
terminal. My initial response was that I would
continue to work each day as I had in the past, for
as long as my health allowed me. I did not feel
there was anything special yet to be done in my
ministry. I then said that I would like to visit my
relatives in northern Italy one last time. Finally,
the answer that was eluding me surfaced in my
mind. It was so simple that I had not yet been able
to put it into words. I told the media that probably the most important thing I could do for the
people of the Archdiocese—and everyone of good
will—would be the way I prepare for death.

This concept began to take shape in my life
in the next few days and weeks. And this book
is an important part of my preparation for

dying and allowing others to share in that awesome experience.

MY MINISTRY CONTINUES

As I NOTED in the introductory meditation to this section, the very next day I went to Saint Barbara Church in Brookfield for a second communal anointing of the sick. How things had changed! I was anointed again, this time as someone preparing for death. It was a deeply spiritual experience for me.

Because I was told that I still had some quality time left, I resolved to continue my pastoral schedule to the extent that I could. As usual, September was a fairly full month. At times, I spoke at two events on the same day. I also continued my cancer ministry, making up to a dozen phone calls each evening and writing notes of encouragement to fellow cancer patients.

On September 9, only ten days after announcing that I had terminal cancer, I received the Medal of Freedom from President Bill Clinton at the White House. I was very humbled to receive the highest honor given to a civilian by our nation.

Aware of my physical condition, the White House graciously scheduled the ceremony, which included eight other recipients, to coincide with a visit to Washington during which I was to give a major address at Georgetown University. The occasion involved considerable walking, and I was glad I'd brought my cane with me. I gave several media interviews on the White House lawn. My address at Georgetown, which was well received, reiterated the need for a consistent ethic of life and emphasized the importance of religion in our society (despite the often-invoked separation of church and state in this country). All in all, it was a very full, exhausting day—but one of the most memorable in my life.

On September 20, I went to Boston to receive the Caritas Christi Medal from the Catholic Healthcare System of the Archdiocese of Boston. I was pleased to be honored in this way for my work on behalf of Catholic healthcare, but I was quite ill during this trip. The new chemotherapy that I was receiving had many more side effects than I had previously experienced. Moreover, the fatigue associated with pancreatic cancer was becoming much more pronounced.

Meeting with the Holy Father

On September 23, I left for Rome to report personally to Pope John Paul II about my health. Ken Velo accompanied me, but I asked the media not to go with me. I had given so many interviews that I was running out of things to say! And the answers to the questions I anticipated—about my visit with the Holy Father—were both personal and confidential. We arranged for a simple "photo op" at the Villa Stritch, but I gave no interviews. The weather was great, and I was able to rest and relax a bit. We were not sure precisely on what day or where the Holy Father would see me.

The Holy Father and I met at Castelgondolfo, the papal summer residence in the Alban Hills near Rome, on Friday, September 27. When we concluded our audience, Monsignor Velo joined us for a few moments.

We had one more day in Italy, so Ken and I traveled to Assisi on Saturday, September 28. We celebrated Mass for all the priests of the Archdiocese and had a delightful lunch with some of the

Franciscan friars there. There was a moment of humor during the Mass. Because we had no congregation, I had decided not to include a Prayer of the Faithful before the offertory. Ken, however, pulled a piece of paper out of his pocket. He said that he had written down several categories of priests for whom we were praying: priests who are infirm, retired, alcoholic, young and vivacious, dispirited, marginal, talented, bilingual or trilingual, in parish work, in special work, in racial and ethnic ministry, confused, in ministry to priests, newly ordained, students, on leave, dysfunctional, happy and contented. At the conclusion of his recital I laughed and noted that I belonged in several categories myself! This visit to Assisi was one of the most wonderful events of these last few months since I learned that I have terminal cancer.

LETTING GO OF THE FUTURE

WHEN KEN AND I RETURNED to Chicago, I resumed my pastoral schedule but found it more and more difficult to carry out. I became driven by the desire to put everything in my life into order.

I finalized my will, made arrangements for distributing my remaining possessions, asked my immediate staff to prepare my and their files for removal to our archdiocesan records and archives center, and made some basic decisions about my funeral. I also finalized arrangements for my mother's continuing care after my death.

PRAYING WITH THE PRESBYTERATE

ON OCTOBER 7, about 800 archdiocesan and religious priests joined me in prayer at Holy Name Cathedral. While no one said it explicitly, I could sense from the many tears that I saw that it was the last time we would gather together while I am alive. I could not help thinking of the evening we had first gathered in prayer in the cathedral—for my canonical installation on August 24, 1982— and I suspect that many of them also recalled that beautiful occasion. So, I decided to repeat the conclusion of my homily on that occasion:

As our lives and ministries are mingled together through the breaking of the Bread and the blessing of the Cup, I hope that long before my name falls from the eucharistic prayer in the silence of death you will know well who I am. You will know because we will work and play together, fast and pray together, mourn and rejoice together, despair and hope together, dispute and be reconciled together. You will know me as a friend, fellow priest, and bishop. You will know also that I love you. For I am Joseph, your brother!

Toward the end of the service, before I blessed them, all the priests raised their hands and blessed me. I doubt there were any eyes without tears at that moment. Mine were filled to the brim!

LETTING GO OF MY MINISTRY

BY MID-OCTOBER IT BECAME quite obvious to me, as my doctor confirmed, that the cancer was spreading more rapidly than we had anticipated. I had been told that the tumors of some patients who received the same chemotherapy I was receiving stopped growing or diminished in size. This was not true of mine, however. Because of this and the side effects of the medication, I decided to stop receiving chemotherapy. The results of the growing tumors are a pervasive fatigue, daily fever, and some chest pain caused by the pressure of some of the tumors on the capsule surrounding the liver. On a recent visit Dr. Gaynor noted that I did not have any jaundice, which often indicates that the pancreatic cancer has spread to the liver. I jokingly told her that maybe some jaundice would be good. Because I continued to look fairly good—especially on television—many people assumed that I was not as sick as I truly was and made many requests—and even demands—of me. Most understood, I trust, why I could not honor their requests, even the persistent ones.

We had planned to hold the first conference of the Catholic Common Ground Project in the spring of 1997. As it became increasingly clear that I would not be able to attend it, we decided to have a meeting of the committee in Chicago on Thursday, October 24. While we had planned on my participation throughout the day, I had to limit my attendance to a morning meeting and an evening address. During the morning meeting I turned over the leadership of the group to my longtime friend and colleague, Archbishop Oscar Lipscomb, Archbishop of Mobile. That evening, I focused on the nature, the importance, and the future of the Catholic Common Ground Project.

Earlier this week, on Tuesday, October 29, I went to the Loyola Medical Center for a special occasion, the dedication of the newly named Cardinal Bernardin Cancer Center. On May 31, almost one year after my surgery, I had been invited back to the hospital to participate in a press conference in which officials of the Medical Center announced plans to rename the Cancer Center in my honor. The Center had originally opened in 1994 and since that time had helped many people like me. With the renaming of the Center, the administrators had launched a fundraising initiative for a $20 million endowment for cancer research and clinical programs.

My fatigue prevented me from doing everything they would have liked me to do last Tuesday. But I offered some impromptu remarks to the medical staff assembled in the new building, thanking them for the wonderful, compassionate, and competent care they had given me. I gave them my blessing, and then I was very moved as all of them raised their hands and voices to bless me.

I spoke briefly to a gathering of supporters to the Center who had been invited to a special dinner in a tent outside the Cancer Center. A violent storm came up, however, with lightning, thunder, and eighty-mile-per-hour winds. The dinner had to be postponed, and most of the guests left early. It was probably my last public appearance in the Archdiocese of Chicago.

THE CROSS COMES INTO CLEAR VIEW

AN MRI THE NEXT DAY confirmed that the cancerous tumors continue to grow. So, yesterday, October 31, I decided to cut back drastically on my public appearances beginning immediately. I also entrusted the day-to-day responsibilities of the Archdiocese to my Vicar General, Bishop Raymond Goedert, who lives with me and Ken Velo.

While this was very difficult for me to do, it was clearly necessary and in the best interests of the Archdiocese. In my homily for the liturgy of my solemn installation as Seventh Archbishop of Chicago, I had reminded the congregation (and the vast television audience) that Jesus, the Good Shepherd, the model for all my ministry,

> is one who lays down his life for his people. Some live this calling literally, shedding their blood as martyrs. Others live it in the unstinting giving of their time, their energy, their very selves to those they have been called to serve. Whatever the future holds for me, I pledge this day to live as a good shepherd who willingly lays down his life for you.

The words are simple and direct, and I meant with all my being what I said. I also added toward the conclusion of the homily:

> If God gives me the strength and grace, I shall preside in charity over the Church in Chicago from the bishop's chair of this cathedral for many years. . . .

Together we may cross the threshold of the third millennium, a milestone for civilization and for Christianity. For however many years I am given, I give myself to you. I offer you my service and leadership, my energies, my gifts, my mind, my heart, my strength, and, yes, my limitations. I offer you myself in faith, hope, and love.

It has become apparent that it is not the Lord's will that you and I cross the threshold of the third millennium together. But in the last fourteen years I have given myself to this local church, the Church in the United States, and the universal Church. I have also shared my life with the broader family of metropolitan Chicago and beyond. Today, while there is still breath in me, I offer you myself in faith, hope, and love as well as in suffering, dying, and peace.

The Gift of Peace

THE GIFT OF PEACE

A S I CONCLUDE THIS BOOK, I am both exhausted and exhilarated. Exhausted because the fatigue caused by the cancer is overwhelming. Exhilarated because I have finished a book that has been very important to me.

As I write these final words, my heart is filled with joy. I am at peace.

It is the first day of November, and fall is giving way to winter. Soon the trees will lose the vibrant colors of their leaves and snow will cover the ground. The earth will shut down, and people will race to and from their destinations bundled up for warmth. Chicago winters are harsh. It is a time of dying.

But we know that spring will soon come with all its new life and wonder.

It is quite clear that I will not be alive in the spring. But I will soon experience new life in a different way. Although I do not know what to expect in the afterlife, I do know that just as God has called me to serve him to the best of my ability throughout my life on earth, he is now calling me home.

Many people have asked me to tell them about heaven and the afterlife. I sometimes smile at the request because I do not know any more than they do. Yet, when one young man asked if I looked forward to being united with God and all those who have gone before me, I made a connection to something I said earlier in this book. The first time I traveled with my mother and sister to my parents' homeland of Tonadico di Primiero, in northern Italy, I felt as if I had been there before. After years of looking through my mother's photo albums, I knew the mountains, the land, the houses, the people. As soon as we entered the valley, I said, "My God, I know this place. I am home." Somehow I think crossing from this life into life eternal will be similar. I will be home.

What I would like to leave behind is a simple prayer that each of you may find what I have found—God's special gift to us all: the gift of peace. When we are at peace, we find the freedom to be most fully who we are, even in the worst of times. We let go of what is nonessential and embrace what is essential. We empty ourselves so that God may more fully work within us. And we become instruments in the hands of the Lord.

As I have said so often, if we seek communion with the Lord, we must pray. One of my favorite prayers is attributed to Saint Francis of Assisi. Let us conclude by reciting it together:

> Lord, make me an instrument of your peace.
> Where there is hatred, let me sow love.
> Where there is injury, pardon.
> Where there is doubt, faith.
> Where there is despair, hope.
> Where there is darkness, light.
> Where there is sadness, joy.
> O Divine Master, grant that I may not
>   so much seek
> to be consoled, as to console;
> to be understood, as to understand;
> to be loved, as to love;
> for it is in giving that we receive,
> it is in pardoning that we are pardoned.
> It is in dying that we are born to eternal life.

PUBLISHER'S
NOTE

JOSEPH CARDINAL BERNARDIN always took great pride in his penmanship. He loved fine pens and stationery, and throughout the course of his life took the time to handwrite countless letters, cards, and notes to people all over the world. Today, many of those writings are framed and hang in the homes of those who want to remember their friend and brother, Joseph Bernardin.

As Cardinal Bernardin finished *The Gift of Peace,* he wanted to reach his readers on a very personal level. He chose to handwrite the letter that begins this book and the titles of the introduction, part openers, meditations, and conclusion.

The Cardinal completed *The Gift of Peace* on November 1, 1996, just thirteen days before he died of pancreatic cancer. His finishing touch was to write the title of the book and sign his name for the front cover.